HOLISTIC TECHNOLOGY INTEGRATION

THE P4 FRAMEWORK FOR PROFESSIONAL DEVELOPMENT

JASON SIKO

ANAPHORA LITERARY PRESS

BROWNSVILLE, TEXAS

Anaphora Literary Press
1898 Athens Street
Brownsville, TX 78520
http://anaphoraliterary.com

Book design by Anna Faktorovich, Ph.D.

Copyright © 2016 by Jason Siko

All rights reserved. No part of this book may be reproduced in any form or by any electronic or mechanical means, including information storage and retrieval systems, without permission in writing from Jason Siko. Writers are welcome to quote brief passages in their critical studies, as American copyright law dictates.

Printed in the United States of America, United Kingdom and in Australia on acid-free paper.

Edited by Catherine Zheng

Published in 2016 by Anaphora Literary Press

Holistic Technology Integration: The P4 Framework for Professional Development

Jason Siko—1st edition.

Library of Congress Control Number: 2016915594

Library Cataloging Information

Siko, Jason, 1975-, author.
   Holistic Technology Integration : The P4 Framework for Professional Development / Jason Siko
   80 p. ; 9 in.
   Includes bibliographical references
   ISBN 978-1-68114-296-8 (softcover : alk. paper)
   ISBN 978-1-68114-297-5 (hardcover : alk. paper)
   ISBN 978-1-68114-298-2 (e-book)
1. Education—Professional Development. 2. Education—Teaching Methods & Materials—Science & Technology. 3. Education—Aims & Objectives. I. Title.
LB2832-2844.1: School administration and organization: Teaching personnel
407 Education, research & related topics

HOLISTIC TECHNOLOGY INTEGRATION

THE P4 FRAMEWORK FOR PROFESSIONAL DEVELOPMENT

JASON SIKO

CONTENTS

Introduction   7
            Provided by the district
            Provided informally
            Before the school year begins
            During the school year
    The Well Connected Teacher
    The P4 Model
    What Lies Ahead

Chapter 1: Professionalism   13
    Personal Learning Network
    Examples of PLN Platforms
        Twitter
        Facebook
        YouTube
        Pinterest
        Blogs and RSS Readers
        Social Bookmarking
        Podcasts
    Conclusion
    Professional Development Activities
    References

Chapter 2: Productivity   27
    Communication
    Collaboration
    Just Ask!
        Email
        Grading/feedback
        Absent Work
        File Organization
        File Sharing
        Passwords
    Distractions
    Conclusions
    Activities
    Performance Improvement without Training
        Information
        Resources

        Capacity
        Incentives
        Motives
    References

Chapter 3: Preferment   43
    The Digital Divide
    1:1/BYOD
    Distance Education
    Blended Learning
    Flipped Learning
    Coding
    Digital Citizenship
    Activities
    References

Chapter 4: Pedagogy   55
    The "Everything Works" Problem
    From Standards to Outcomes
    Pioneers, Skeptics, and Cynics
    The Role of Technology
    Justifying Technology
    Was it Worth it?
    Concluding Thoughts
    References

Conclusion   69
    Putting it all Together
        Analyze Learners
        Determine Performance Gaps
        Determine Target Group(s)
        Align Goals to Decrease Gaps
        Determine Strategies and Interventions
        Develop Data Collection Strategies and Timelines
        Implement Strategies
        Collect and Analyze Formative Data
        Summative Data Collection
    Documenting Teacher Effectiveness

Final Thoughts   76

Introduction

Simple can be harder than complex: You have to work hard to get your thinking clean to make it simple. But it's worth it in the end because once you get there, you can move mountains.
—Steve Jobs

I view K-12 teacher professional development (PD), particularly the use of technology in education, through a unique lens. I taught high school science for over 10 years, but I was informally known as a 'techy' teacher, and was often called upon to deliver training sessions on PD days during the school year. I currently teach both undergraduate and graduate students about technology integration.

My latest position has allowed me to spend far more time researching technology integration. More importantly, it has given me the opportunity to hear stories from teachers across many disciplines and districts about the good, the bad, and the ugly aspects of technology. There are some differences in opinions about what the worst problems of technology are, but common issues include:

- Technology being poorly used by teachers and students
- Technology not showing results
- A lack of data on results
- Terrible professional development

Given that both graduate and undergraduate enrollment in education is currently a major concern (the reasons why are outside of the scope of this text), much of what teachers learn to stay current in their fields (content, grade level, technology, special needs, etc.) is provided:

a) by the district,
b) informally (read: potentially incorrect or misleading)
c) because the teacher is well connected, or
d) not provided.

Let's tackle each of these briefly.

Provided by the district

An old joke about PD goes something like this: if you want to know the agenda for next month's professional development (or even a staff meeting), just read last month's issue of "Educational Leadership". As we'll discuss in later chapters, time is a scarce resource in K-12 education. This not only applies to teachers, but to administrators as well. Furthermore, human resource development in K-12 is often nonexistent. While training departments are the norm in corporate America, with separate human resource departments for management and development, only the former department is present in school districts, and the person in charge likely doesn't come from an education background. As such, professional development in-house is often poorly executed.

Provided informally

Teachers are known for their love of learning, so it doesn't come as a surprise that many teachers take the initiative to develop on their own. They attend conferences, engage in summer self-improvement, and participate in other activities that provide them with useful skills. However, suppose that a corporation let all their employees learn on their own. Would the corporation trust them to stay on task? Would they acknowledge their employee's endeavors?

In some instances, schools do. States provide various levels of licensure based on experience and academic achievement. Salary scales often also take degrees into account. However, though tuition increases at rates that outstrip inflation, teacher salaries remain stagnant. This means that the aforementioned salary bumps are far less valuable, and so teachers that develop by themselves are becoming less and less common.

Finally, conferences, particularly those that focus on technology, tend to devolve into techno-centric cheerleading rallies, where fads, buzzwords, and apps du jour rule the day. Very few sessions end by quantifying the good that technology has done: there are no descriptions of percentage increases in test scores (not that scores should be the only benchmark), or graphs depicting increases in STEM course enrollments in high school (based on "maker" or coding initiatives in elementary school). There isn't even data on how fitness tracking apps, when combined with nutritional changes in the school lunch program, might reduce absences during peak flu season. While ideas flow heavily, many throughts are here today, gone tomorrow.

The final option is providing no professional development. This is more common than one might think. Just like how students drop out because of cognitive differences that start much earlier than many may perceive, teachers often approach professional development with zero interest. Some of that disinterest is due to scheduling.

Before the school year begins

PD is often crammed into the first week or so before students return. Teachers come back well rested, but are then thrust into the spotlight, scurrying to get their classroom ready for students. It's like a first trip to the gym in January after a month of sedation and overindulgence. Hearing about the new initiatives often elicits groans, as many are reminded of the inertia from last year's "new initiatives", which likely ground to a halt by mid-February. Additionally, many ideas are half-baked to begin with (see previous commentary on PD and conferences), with no factual evidence of their effectiveness.

During the school year

Because many communities see public education first and foremost as affordable day care, PD is often delivered on schedules convenient to the community. This often takes the form of PD days scheduled for days close to school breaks, or on 'comp' days next to conferences. Unlike other professions, which allow employees to schedule training around meetings and just "get up and leave", teachers have students to attend to. As a result, the school needs to hire substitute teachers, and teachers need to provide lesson plans, creating extra work for the teacher, and costing the school a substantial amount. Thus, many schools have PD days next to Thanksgiving or Christmas break, or at the end of a week of conferences.

Think about that for a second. Teachers are humans, with lives and families. How focused are they really going to be the day before a break? About as focused as kids the day before a break! How willing are they going to be to spend a day learning about something new (and possibly unproven or unsubstantiated) after a week of work and multiple three-hour parent-teacher meetings? PD days like the one around Memorial Day weekend, when the school year is a week or two from finishing, are particularly tedious.

The Well Connected Teacher

A well connected teacher realizes that for professional development to "stick" it has to be meaningful to his or her work context. A school district can have anywhere from tens to thousands of teachers. Given the differences in content areas and technological acumen, it is nearly impossible for a school district to specifically meet each teacher's needs.

However, it is possible to 'teach teachers to fish'. First, teachers can be given the means to frame their Personal Learning Network, and then learn to 'fish' for their own professional development. Secondly, in order to use technology effectively, teachers need to be pedagogical experts. The idea of technological skill being secondary to pedagogical skill is a concept that will be discussed further in Chapter 4.

The alternative to these options is no professional development. I think anyone who opens this book would agree that professionals who do not improve their knowledge and skills will face disastrous outcomes. A doctor who only utilizes techniques from the medical school they attended in the 1980's, for example, would eventually be sued for malpractice. Designers and engineers who *only* use old materials for their products, rather than new plastics and specialty steels, would find themselves lagging behind their competitors in terms of quality and performance.

However, notice the word *only* in the previous paragraph. Although we want to progress and improve, we must not dismiss the past as outdated and archaic. Great teachers existed well before Saints Steven and Bill plunked their Apples and PCs in classrooms.

The P4 Model

This book focuses on the following model:

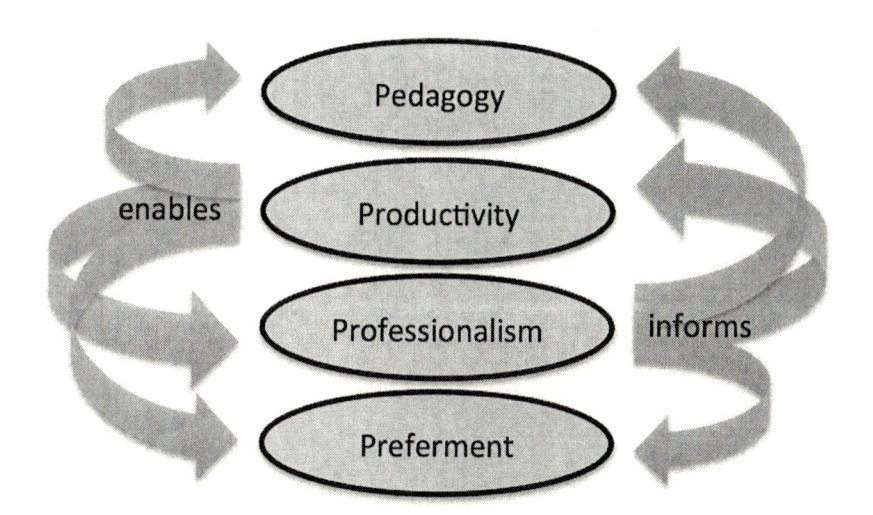

```
           Pedagogy
enables   Productivity
         Professionalism   informs
           Preferment
```

This model will attempt to accomplish several goals. First, it will attempt to create 'fishers of PD'; that is, to have teachers take ownership of their professional development. This is done through Professionalism and Productivity—providing teachers with the skills and knowledge needed to EFFICIENTLY expand their knowledge base and create a network of peers (Chapters 1 and 2). Second, it is an attempt to 'fad-proof' teaching. This is accomplished by relating technology decisions to pedagogy (Chapter 4), as well as providing teachers with an understanding of the underlying currents in educational technology (Chapter 3).

What Lies Ahead

Each chapter will provide an overview of the topic, and examples and discussion of the relevant ideas in each portion of the model will be provided. Overlap between the chapters will be also be discussed. Finally, each chapter will conclude with a set of suggestions for implementing professional development tactics related to each of the four topics. However, this book will not provide information about the technical aspects of the tools and ideas discussed. This was a design decision on my part because I know that once I publish this book, one of the tools discussed will either a) disappear, b) start charging for services once offered for free, or c) radically change its appearance, thus rendering any images in the book outdated and obsolete. What these suggested activities will do is provide ideas on how to successfully implement professional development activities throughout the year—it is not intended to be a one-off, 20 minute, "how-to" session that is doomed to fail.

Chapter 1

Professionalism

What is a *profession*? How do we separate it from a *trade*, a *craft*, or just a plain old *job*? Finn (1953) described a profession as having:

1. an intellectual technique
2. an application of that technique to the practical affairs of man
3. a period of long training necessary before entering into the profession
4. an association of the members of the profession into closely-knit group with a high quality of communication between members
5. a series of standards and a statement of ethics which is enforced
6. an organized body of intellectual theory constantly expanding by research. (p. 232).

Debating whether teaching is a profession (versus a craft, art, science, etc.) is beyond the scope of this book. However, these characteristics, particularly #3, #4, and #6, shine a light on a major problem with educators. Simply put, teachers do not talk to each other, and researchers do not do a good job of sharing research with practitioners.

The cause of these problems, for the most part, is not teachers themselves (the exception is Hattie's 2008 finding that less than 10% of lunchroom talk is about instruction and learning). To explain the first issue with teacher discussion, consider the following. Teaching can be an incredibly isolating profession. A teacher is often the only adult in the room, and often the only one (or one of a small number) with the specific job description of teaching a particular grade or subject. The size of the school may matter (e.g., a school may only have one 4th grade teacher), but not always. In my own experience, during my last 3 years in a high school setting there were 90 teachers and almost 2000 students, I was the only teacher for at least one of my subjects, and for at least one year I was the only teacher for both courses I taught. Even if our school had amenities like common planning time or delayed starts for professional development and data analysis, I would have still not had anyone with whom to collaborate.

Since schools often have limited budgets and resources, attending conferences is becoming a more difficult method of staying current. Annual conferences are often just one-time opportunities to interact and learn from others. On a similar note, professional organizations have associated costs of membership. Although this may include journal subscriptions throughout the year, only a small percentage of articles are applicable to a teacher's specific situation (grade, subject, content, availability of resources for the lesson, etc.). Covering multiple content areas and coverage (local, state, and national organizations) becomes cost prohibitive.

In terms of research informing practice (#6 on the list), there is little in the way of incentives to open channels between educational researchers and practitioners. Teacher access to academic journals is usually limited to the time when they are working on an advanced degree. From a researcher's standpoint, there is little incentive to share their research with practitioners. Despite the common mantra of "publish or perish," tenure-track faculty focus on publishing in peer journals and not practitioner journals, as the latter often isn't counted as a publication for promotion and tenure. Complicating the issue even more is the lack of quality resources accessible for teachers; research is often watered down and over-simplified, containing overreaching claims that are not supported by researchers. Worse, profiteers and charlatans use headline-grabbing studies to support whatever they are selling.

Long story short, there is a lack of communication both between practitioners and between researchers and practitioners. Looking at the definition of a profession at the beginning of the chapter, communication is a key component. How, then, can we leverage technology for communication? How can we teach teachers to be better professionals through the use of technology?

Personal Learning Network

Teacher educators and leaders need to encourage teachers to seek out knowledge rather than expect it from their leaders. Teachers leaving a pre-service preparation program should have the tools to continue to learn outside of the classroom. Veteran teachers need the ability to continue their learning and access just-in-time learning. This is the goal of a Personal Learning Network, or PLN.

A PLN is not a specific application or tool; rather, it is the notion of leveraging various internet resources, specifically Web 2.0 tools and social media, for learning. At this stage, many teachers are familiar with these tools, but some teachers may be dismissive of them. They may feel that these resources won't increase their teaching knowledge. Thus, when providing instruction or professional development, it is crucial to engage teachers and convince them that this process is effective. Let's take a look at the terms in phrase PLN.

- *Personal*—this is fairly straightforward; a PLN is unique to the learner. Educators can customize what content they receive in their newsfeed, stream, etc. They can utilize whatever platform or platforms they choose. They can mix personal and professional content (within reason, of course). Finally, they can "prune" their sources over time as their interests and habits change.
- *Learning*—again, quite straightforward. The purpose of the PLN is TO LEARN. Educators, as professionals, need to stay current on a variety of topics related to their field, whether it be content, pedagogy, legislation, legal issues, technology, labor, politics, or other local or national issues and trends in the field.
- *Network*—this term is perhaps the most ignored of the three. The term network implies something more than a one-way flow of information. While educators who are initially building their PLN may not feel comfortable sharing professional information, eventually they should. Remember, we are professionals, and that means the sharing of knowledge requires a give and take process...or at least the possibility of sharing. In

other words, you cannot share what you do not post!

Examples of PLN Platforms

In this section, we will examine a few different platforms for building a PLN. This examination will be intentionally small in scope. The nature of technology and the internet is quickly changing, and I do not want this book to become obsolete six months after publication. Thus, we will limit our discussion to a few platforms deemed "too big to fail"; that is, services that are established and unlikely to go away anytime soon.

Twitter

Twitter is the likely starting point for a teacher building a PLN. It is a quick way to connect with educational experts as well as other subject-area and grade level colleagues. Twitter is great for asking questions, spurring discussions, and sharing links to valuable information. However, Twitter is often criticized for its overabundance of pointless banter and shameless self-promotion (although other sites, such as Instagram, are shouldering some of that load nowadays). Therefore, teachers may be skeptical of its use. Those arguments are very valid, and to encourage its use as an informal learning platform, technology coaches and leaders should take the time to teach educators about several key features that enhance the learning power of the platform.

First, while not necessarily a feature, it is important to find 'smart' individuals on Twitter. This can begin with a quick Google search (or whatever the preferred search engine may be). It can be something as simple as looking up (without quotes) "Teachers on Twitter," "[content area] teachers on Twitter," or, "educators to follow on Twitter." A quick survey of the search results should help teachers find an initial wave of 'smart' educators to follow. An extension of this activity is to look and see what other people are following. This initial search can lead teachers 'down the rabbit-hole' and allow them to find other helpful people and sites.

The second feature is a hashtag search. The hashtag (i.e., the # symbol, also known as the pound sign, number sign, or octothorpe) is a function in Twitter that adds a searchable label to a tweet. Thus, searching for tweets with the label "#pbl" would return results where people, regardless of whether you follow them or not, have posted something related to PBL, the acronym for project-based learning. Like using a search engine, searching hashtags can provide an educator with a plethora of links, thoughts, and ideas about a particular topic.

A third and related feature in Twitter is Twitter chat (which can also be called a Tweetup). These are chats held at particular times (e.g., Wednesdays at 8pm EST) where a group of people meet to discuss a particular topic. There's usually a moderator who leads the discussion, and all participants respond to questions and comments with posts containing a particular hashtag. For example, in my home state of Michigan, there is a weekly chat that uses the hashtag #miched. Thus, every participant uses that hashtag when talking with one another. Again, a simple Google search ("chemistry twitter chats") should help educators locate relevant chats to follow and/or participate.

There are several benefits to this protocol. First, you can simply follow the chat (i.e., be a nonparticipant, also known as a "lurker") by searching and following the hashtag for the chat. Second, you can interact with people who you may or may not be already following; you have an opportunity to meet new people and network with them.

A final feature that teachers can use on Twitter for learning purposes is an aggregator. Aggregators, such as HootSuite or TweetDeck, allow people to customize their Twitter platform so that they can organize and follow multiple streams. Individuals can create a column that displays information from their primary feed, lists (where certain people are organized into subgroups), and specific hashtags. This type of organization allows people to distinguish between personal and professional interests, which gives educators the ability to utilize social media for both work and entertainment purposes.

Facebook

Facebook seems like an unlikely candidate for learning. Many educators believe that a strong presence on Facebook is detrimental to their careers. One only needs to check recent news stories about teachers friending students (and what follows) or teachers getting fired for statements or pictures posted on this site to support this negative sentiment. However, because over one billion people are on the site, it cannot be ignored.

This fact has not eluded professional education associations. Be it the teachers' unions (NEA, AFT, and their state affiliates), state and national content area organizations, or technology groups—countless professional groups have a presence on Facebook. In the past, organizations used to use separate and closed social networks (and some still do), but it is counterproductive to make users learn an additional login and password, let alone take the time to log into an additional site and learn its navigation idiosyncrasies. Therefore, many organizations simply created group pages on Facebook that both members and non-members can join (larger organizations are more likely to be open since the task of vetting membership requests would be overwhelming).

Since many educators are on Facebook, the site can serve two purposes. First, it can become a networking avenue for teachers to connect with one another. It may even serve as a job posting board. With respect to learning, groups can post news and information relevant to one's teaching assignment, labor issues, legislation, and so on. Only a minority of these posts would require a teacher to log into the association website (where an active membership is required), and so these resources are usually free.

Again, it is not my intent to discourage membership in an association. As the saying goes, "membership has its privileges." However, teachers would need to join an incredibly large number of organizations to cover every aspect of their job description, and membership fees would soon become prohibitively expensive. Therefore, they can instead leverage PLN to keep current in multiple arenas while keeping costs down. For example, my background is in science education. I was a biology and chemistry teacher for 13 years. I also have a Master's degree in Futures Studies, and my Ph.D. is in Instructional Technology. Here is a partial list of organizations I have belonged to in the past 20 years:

- National Science Teachers Association
- Michigan Science Teachers Association
- International Society for Technology in Education
- Michigan Association for Computer Users in Learning
- World Future Society
- Association of Professional Futurists
- Association for the Advancement of Computing in Education
- Association for Educational Communications and Technology
- American Educational Research Association

Fees for these organizations range from $50 to $200 annually. To maintain membership in all of these would cost me over $1000 annually. For a teacher, membership in a state and national level content organization, plus a state and national technology organization, could reach $250 annually. In this day and age, given current teacher salaries, it is unreasonable to expect teachers to pay this much. I belong to a few of these organizations and follow others—like my state's principal association—on Twitter or other social media. While I'm not an administrator, I find that online groups provide the best information and insight into educational policy and legislation at the state level.

YouTube

YouTube is more than just cat videos. Like Facebook, the site is highly utilized by content area associations for messages, news, and information. Museums, colleges/universities, and topic enthusiasts also post informative content. An often overlooked feature of YouTube is the ability to subscribe to a user's channel so that you are notified when they post a new video. Just like Twitter and Facebook, this can be an information source that automatically appears in your PLN when something new is presented, rather than having to hunt down and search for interesting content. One word of caution when using YouTube:

consider the source. While the NSTA (National Science Teachers' Organization) YouTube channel is clearly legitimate, joethescienceguy's channel may contain incorrect information. One quality video may be followed by several duds. In cases like this, read the About section of the channel to learn more about the person, and do a quick Google search to see if any other information can be found.

Pinterest

Just like how YouTube is more than just funny cat videos, Pinterest is more than just arts and crafts, recipes, and Mason jar salad tips. Pinterest has become a repository for sharing classroom ideas, including lesson plans. Also, like YouTube, Twitter, and Facebook, professional organizations understand the power of social media and have a presence on Pinterest as well. Educators can use Pinterest in ways similar to the previously mentioned platforms; educators should look for their professional organizations, and vet (i.e., do some research on) channels that lack credentials.

Blogs and RSS Readers

Blogs (originally referred to as weblogs) are easy-to-use sites that are essentially public journals that allow people to share their thoughts and ideas with an online audience. Readers can comment on blogs, and many educators have their own blogs, where they openly discuss topics from their classroom (lessons, handling difficult situations, and so on). Bloggers often connect with one another and form relationships, thus creating a professional support network. They comment on each other's posts, and promote other bloggers on their own blogs. Sometimes, educators will try to monetize their blogs through ad support, or branch out into the world of consulting; their blog then becomes a way to promote their services.

In addition to blogs, there are plenty of education and entertainment websites that teachers visit on a consistent basis. We often check a website to see if there is any new information, only to find that it hasn't been updated since our last visit. Wouldn't it be nice if there were a way to streamline this visitation process—a way to ensure that we're notified when new information is posted?

There is. Welcome to the world of RSS readers. RSS stands for several different things, but is primarily known as Rich Site Summary. Blogs and other websites create an RSS feed containing brief information about updates (like new posts) along with an image or preview of the update. Readers can be web-based or mobile—on a device like a phone or tablet. Instead of checking a bunch of websites daily, people can access new information in one place.

Finding blogs is, once again, a simple Google search away. Once you find an interesting blog, and set up a RSS reader, you can simply add the URL of the blog to your reader, and voila… you will be automatically notified when it is updated. Now, many people do receive email updates when sites are updated. The advantage of RSS readers, however, is that RSS updates are separated from email messages, which prevents you from becoming distracted by a new blog post while doing work. RSS feeds also often show previews of the content, so you can quickly scroll through all of your feeds, read the title or the first paragraph, and decide whether to read the rest of the post or article. A final benefit of RSS readers is that they put all of your interests in one spot, so you don't have to check 20 or more websites for updates—those 20 or more websites (and any new information) come to you.

Social Bookmarking

Have you ever bookmarked a website on your browser, phone, or tablet, and been unable to remember the website name when you were away from that particular device? Have you ever felt that emailing links to your staff or department was a futile effort, because many of your colleagues would likely delete the message while attempting to keep their inbox in control? Just posting a link to Twitter may not show others why they should read it, and there isn't a great way to organize tweeted links. Fortunately, social bookmarking provides a solution to these problems—it allows you to share and curate information collected on the internet.

Social bookmarking sites, such as Diigo and Delicious, provide different levels of usage. At their most basic level, they allow users to store links they can access from any device, either by logging into the bookmarking site, using browser plug-ins, or opening a mobile app. They also allow users to curate their bookmarks through a system of tags. For example, I could tag personal bookmarks as "personal", but also add multiple tags related to various courses, topics, or units (e.g., ChemCom, Materials, recycling). If I needed to look for something specific that I tagged a long time ago, I could search by tags rather than scroll through hundreds, if not thousands, of bookmarks.

Aside from tags, social bookmarking sites allow you to annotate entries—write a few sentences summarizing the information to remind yourself why you bookmarked the site in the first place. Further, some sites (like Diigo) actually save a copy of the webpage, and allow the user to highlight and add comments on the page.

From a social standpoint, users can create networks to share specific bookmarks or to collaboratively collect information. If I find a resource that I know I am unlikely to use, but I know someone who can use that resource, I can share it with his or her account. Using tags, I can create a network of all of the ChemCom teachers (in my district or region) and give everyone in that network access to the links I saved for a particular topic. In addition, if you annotate the link or highlight pieces of a site, that information can be shared as well. So, rather than simply emailing a link, you also explain what is useful about it, as well as specifically where to look on the site.

Podcasts

Podcasts are downloadable audio "shows" that can be listened to at your convenience, and on your computer, tablet, or mobile device. Once a podcast is downloaded, you can listen to it anywhere: at home, at work, at the gym, or on the road (if your car stereo can connect to your device). Podcasts are generally updated on a consistent basis; weekly or biweekly, for example. Your device can be set to automatically download new episodes; like blogs and RSS readers, you do not have to continually hunt for updates. Like many of the other resources discussed in this chapter, a quick internet search for "top education podcasts," "math podcasts," etc., is a good starting point. Further, podcast distribution services such as iTunes rank their podcasts based on downloads, so a search within the app under "Education" should yield excellent results.

Conclusion

The purpose of this chapter is to demonstrate several ways to leverage technology to increase the professional behavior of teaching staff. In particular, these tools provide ways to overcome the lack of communication between staff and with teachers and experts outside of the school walls. There is going to be some overlap between this chapter and the next chapter on productivity. However, this chapter is focused more on creating networks and channels for teachers to both communicate and stay current. Most importantly, most of the proposed changes are free, or provide quite a bit of functionality for free (some of the tools provide increased capabilities for an increased fee).

However, simply telling teachers about these tools, or even showing them how to set up accounts with each of these services, will not ensure that they learn. In order to change the culture of a building or district, school or district leaders must decide on specific outcomes, and set measurable goals for teachers after a year or more of developing and building a PLN. This can range from administering simple reaction surveys at the end of the year, to giving teachers and administrators a voice in the regional, state, or national debate on educational topics. The latter option emphasizes the development of staff PLNs as an option focused on sharing information rather than passively consuming it.. Regardless, if there are no goals, there will be no results.

And finally, I would be remiss if I did not circle back to the last letter in PLN: Network. Consider the following steps in shifting teachers from simply consuming to creating and sharing ideas as well.

Step 1—Consume

- Build your PLN
- Make it a habit to read and follow
- LEARN
- Update/prune connections
- Streamline (focus on a few platforms that work for you)

Step 2—Communicate

- Talk to the people you follow
- Respond to questions and inquiries
- Expand and grow your network

Step 3—Create

- Start and contribute to discussions
- Create and maintain your own (blog, YouTube channel, podcast)
- TELL YOUR STORY!

What follows, as is the case with each chapter of the book, are a series of activities and plans for developing this aspect of the model with staff.

Professional Development Activities

1. An obvious professional development activity is providing information on tools to use as well as time to set up accounts. Instructors must be slow and deliberate when explaining how to use various tools and walking teachers through the setup process. Technology leaders should rely heavily on their tech-savvy staff, following a 'diffusion of innovation' model, where primary leaders get early adopters up and running. These early adopters can assist teachers who need more technical assistance during the setup process.
2. Once the setup is complete, instructors should give staff time

to explore. One assignment I use with my students is to have them find 30 different sources for their PLN. There are several caveats to this assignment. First, they must spread these resources out over three different platforms—they cannot simply find 30 people to follow on Twitter. They must learn to operate in multiple platforms. Secondly, they cannot 'double dip.' In other words, they cannot follow the same person on Twitter and Pinterest (or follow their blog or YouTube channel).

3. Allow time for sharing. This should occur several weeks to months after the initial PD session. Provide some time during department or staff meetings for educators to reflect upon and share their experiences. However, some structure to this activity should be provided, and this shouldn't be a free-for-all share session. For example, faculty might be encouraged to share specific things they learned, connections they made, and, most importantly, how their PLN contributed to student success.

4. Allow time for 'pruning'—choosing certain platforms to use more frequently. Given all of the various avenues, people will naturally gravitate towards one or more platforms. I primarily use an RSS reader, along with Twitter. Also, an individual's initial choice of who to follow may not be as useful as they originally thought. Providing time for this activity also allows educators to explore further options once the initial "herd" of potential sites has been thinned.

5. Model good practice. Allocate particular times for people to check their PLN, similar to a required reading time. Quick emails (or better yet, posts to social networks) within connected groups such as, "I started following @[somebody] on Twitter. Really good information," will keep the PLN concept on the front burner.

6. Arrange meetups with other groups or important people who are popular on social networks. If working with another building or district, build rapport by scheduling time for face-to-face interaction to solidify relationships. If a prominent educational expert is in the area, arrange for an informal meeting (on or off school grounds) to simply chat. Once again, meetings with others will improve the quality of digital relationships.

References

Finn, J. (1953). Professionalizing the audio-visual field. In D. P. Ely & Plomp T. (Eds.), *Classic Writings on Instructional Technology* (Vol. 1, pp. 231—241). Englewood, CO: Libraries Unlimited, Inc.

Hattie, J. (2008). *Visible learning: A synthesis of over 800 meta-analyses relating to achievement.* New York: Routledge.

Chapter 2

Productivity

Educators often complain about their lack of time. Once the school year begins, teachers, even well intentioned ones, tend to burn through their seed corn and have trouble keeping up with grading, lesson planning, and other tasks associated with their job. As a result, teachers may see technology integration as just another item to add to their list of things to do. At that point, most professional development on technology is futile, because it is seen as another mandate that teachers are not given the proper resources (i.e., funding, compensation, or time allotment) to carry out.

Therefore, one of the major challenges of technology professional development is to get educators to understand that this initial extra work increases their own efficiency (read: allow them to get their heads above water), making their job easier. It should also benefit student performance in the classroom, a topic that will be covered further in Chapter 4. However, it is important to illustrate what benefits teachers can gain from technology professional development so they will buy into the system.

The rationale for this approach is rooted in andragogy, or adult learning theory. Malcolm Knowles's theory of adult learning lists six traits of adult learners that should drive professional development initiatives. They are:

1. The learner's need to know
2. Self-concept of the learner
3. Prior experience of the learner
4. Readiness to learn
5. Orientation to learning, and
6. Motivation to learn (Knowles, Holton & Swanson, 2005, p. 3)

When we look at activities at the end of the chapter, pay particular attention to the section that focuses on understanding the needs of staff, and strive to not only plan, but to communicate that you are addressing their workplace needs.

One of the major hurdles when teaching technology professional development is getting staff buy in. Although you are promising that what you are teaching should save them time and/or lead to higher student achievement in the long run, development requires teachers to dedicate a substantial amount of their own time. Since teachers already believe they're short on time, it will be difficult to convince them to spend more time learning about a tool or technique, setting up an account, or altering their current procedural and instructional practices to integrate the technology into their daily routine. Teachers may also feel that their current instruction is adequate; that they have the results they want and any lack of achievement is due to their students, and thus out of their control.

Compare this situation to road construction. Road construction is a necessary headache. Roads deteriorate over time, and drivers feel the effects of a road that is falling apart, but no one wants to be faced with the inconvenience of taking an alternate route or dealing with lane restrictions. We wish all of the construction would happen during the night without us noticing, with the barrels and lane restrictions taken down every day before we begin our commute.

Departments of transportation often employ signs that empathize with drivers. Mixed in with advisory signs are signs that say things such as, "Short term delays lead to long term relief." Though these are correct statements, they do not assuage drivers stuck in traffic on a Monday morning when they're late for work. This is the same problem faced by those designing professional development. Selling the fact that this disruption and subsequent time requirements is key to the success of the program.

One way to view productivity is to split it into two different areas. The first involves the routines and procedures that everyone must do. This can include the gradebook, attendance program, student information system, content/learning management system, and anything else considered an integral part of the teacher's life.

Since these are generally routine operations, teachers may need some initial help and instruction, but after that, most of the help should be in the form of just-in-time job aids and assistance. In the case of the latter, consider having both a help desk/call-in center. For the former, paper and online documentation should be vigilantly kept up-to-date, with easy access to a FAQ section. Finally, these routine operations can be addressed in emails and staff meetings (e.g., a Tech Tips minute). A building or district technology advisory committee should be in charge of developing and maintaining the documentation in conjunction with the IT staff.

The second avenue for increasing productivity is specifically addressing the needs of the building, department (or grade level) and individual teachers. Addressing these needs requires learner participation and buy in; therefore, it is necessary to communicate with the staff about their specific needs. This should be addressed throughout the year but also at the end of the school year in preparation for PD development for the following school year.

With respect to productivity, we are looking to streamline operations to make teachers' lives easier. Some of these are addressed in the chapter on Professionalism, so there is some overlap. However, we need to first examine the routine tasks of teachers.

Communication

In a faculty meeting recently, a fellow colleague mentioned that she put directions for students on how to properly communicate with her in her syllabus. While some initially scoffed at the notion, in the end, her purpose was two-fold. First, it communicates to her students the expectations regarding proper conduct between students and teachers. Second, it makes her life easier, as it increases the quality of the communication and reduces the time she spends on her email.

Keep in mind this is a college scenario, where her students are twenty-somethings—adults. Also keep in mind that email conduct is taught in the private sector as well. So, some initial discussion about generational differences, particularly when communication media are concerned, is quite justified. This is one aspect of communication: creating a method that is clear, concise, and consistent for teachers, students, administrators, and, if possible, parents.

The second aspect is organization. Professional development regarding your district's email system is key to streamlining the communication process. This can be more procedural in nature (see above), such as sending attachments, setting up folders, prioritizing messages, etc.

The third aspect is not so much technical as it is habit and mindset. The actual process and performance of communication through electronic means can be streamlined to increase efficiency. Examples of this include how many times per day we should check email, whether we should we leave our email program running at all times, how to address issues in terms of ease, importance, and so on.

Collaboration

Teachers, from what I have observed, tend to have a bit of a perfectionist streak. They often like to have things "just right," meaning, "just how I like it." While I'm usually the first to ask for research supporting such claims, I would posit that being the person in charge of children every day tends to make teachers feel slightly superior. Thus, while sharing the workload may appeal to some, the driving urge to avoid compromise (i.e., having something not exactly the way you intended) may override common sense for teachers.

There are other hurdles that stand in the way of teachers collaborating with one another. Arranging common planning time with colleagues is next to impossible. Teachers have commitments both before and after school; schedules, family obligations, students coming for help, etc. Most importantly, teachers must maintain order and address the needs of their own captive audience; they simply cannot walk away from their classroom to go work with a colleague.

Thus, collaboration needs to be asynchronous as well as synchronous. Technology can play a role in this, but often teachers resort to the most convenient tool available—email. Email is by far the WORST way to collaborate. It is incredibly easy to get things out of order, have multiple people going off in different directions, and the process and problems dis-incentivizes collaboration in general.

Two useful collaboration tools are wikis and Google Docs. They allow for asynchronous collaboration, have discussion and chat features, save previous versions that can be restored, have varying levels of access (full editing, comment only, and view only), and can handle the addition of media beyond simple text. Both have their minor advantages and disadvantages, so here are a few considerations:

Will most of the collaboration be asynchronous? If so, then either is fine. Where wikis can come up short is when there will be plenty of synchronous collaboration. Most wikis have a "save page" option, and if two people are working on a page simultaneously, then some changes can get lost. Wikis also have a discussion feature, but lack a solid real-time chat feature.

How much media will be in the document? Google Docs support the addition of images and video, but if the final product is meant to be very media rich, wikis tend to be more aesthetically pleasing.

Is the document meant for public or private use (i.e., do we everyone to see the final product)? If the final product is public, using a wiki may be better suited for a website-like display. If the product is internally shared, then a Google Doc may be a better choice.

Again, this is a limited list, and depending on the products that you can access, may influence your decision. Finally, documents are not the only way to collaborate. Google Sites, which also can function like a wiki, are useful for building course web pages. Presentations can be built collaboratively using Google Slides or Prezis. Research and idea sharing can occur through social bookmarking tools (Diigo and Delicious).

Finally, for larger projects with multiple moving parts, a project management tool may be useful for projects that involve revising curricula or organizing large, school-wide initiatives. Aside from document sharing, these tools allow for the creation of task lists, delegation, and progress charts. Free, online project management tools like Asana are currently available for anyone to use.

Just Ask!

Unfortunately, I cannot provide a definitive list of tools or procedures, since every district or school has unique needs and IT resources. The productivity aspect also requires teacher input. Simply ask, "what are your biggest time drags?" and then provide professional development on how to make those tasks easier. My 10+ years in the classroom would suggest the following:

Email

There are basically two types of people in the world: those with inboxes containing fewer than 50 emails, and those with inboxes with 10,000 or more emails. Email consumes us. Many teachers keep their email program open during the day. Every time they hear a "ding" or see a notification, it distracts them from their current focus. However, the alternative—setting aside one specific time of day for email—is somewhat impractical for teachers. Before school? No way; teachers are too busy prepping for the day. Conference hour or recess? Possibly; but likewise, there's more pressing things to do. After school? Kids needing help trump sitting at a computer.

Regardless, choices need to be made and setting aside certain periods of time strictly for email is a key component to getting through the day. Now, what about that already bloated inbox? Teachers will likely not have the time or willpower to clean out their inboxes in one day. So, a strategy must be in place in order to chip away at this problem. This can be approached much like credit card debt—teachers should put strategies in place to stop the problem from growing while simultaneously working to reduce the problems that have already accumulated. In the case of the former, exploring email providers options for prioritizing email, directing it into folders, and various other productivity tricks (like a "two minutes or less" rule that some experts promote) would work. In the latter case, setting aside some time each week to delete or organize 50 or so emails would be effective. This problem won't go away overnight, but over time, it will become more manageable.

Grading/feedback

Much of this will be covered in Chapter 4. However, I will say this: feedback is one of THE most important aspects of increasing student achievement (Hattie, 2008). The most important elements of feedback are amount (more is better), quality (more detail is better), and turn-around time. Delayed feedback should be diminished, to help students understand new material that builds on prior mastery. The problem is that adhering to the first two elements, amount and quality, will take time.

Absent Work

Related to grading and feedback is the constant need to address student needs because of absenteeism (past or future). This can include students coming back from an absence, students telling you they are going to be absent, and parents emailing you about these same things. Possible solutions are one-part behaviorism and one-part technology.

File Organization

Part of being efficient when it comes to technology involves knowing where to find things. Providing some help with organizing folders and files on a computer or server can go a long way towards preventing teachers from getting bogged down. More importantly, it would be a good idea to provide time for "spring cleaning"; that is, a time to purge old and unused files from hard drives and servers. Memory can become scarce very quickly these days. Though drive spaces have become larger, so have assignment file sizes. Instead of only documents, most of which are under 200K, a classroom set of student created videos can get unruly very fast.

A simple file structure for class documents would look as basic as this:

Course (or grade) → Unit → Topic

Of course, a folder for general documents for each course (syllabus, curriculum guide, etc.) would be present as well. Also, if there are digital 'hoarders' among you, suggest a folder labeled "old" for things that are no longer used in classes but are simply too good to destroy, or backup documents on an external drive.

For grading, it might look like this:

Year → Class/Hour

Finally, a folder for school related items, and a (hopefully small) folder to keep any personal documents should be created.

File Sharing

Again, part of the issue with the "old way"—emailing things back and forth between colleagues—is the difficulty of keeping track of the most recent version of a document. Using cloud-based services can help with this problem. For teachers with access to Google Apps for Education (GAFE), professional development should center on how to share folders and collaborate on documents.

Other file sharing services can also be useful. However, many of the free versions of these services are limited in size (GAFE is also limited in size, but it is often sufficient for teacher's work). Also, unlike GAFE, these services are limited to sharing files and commenting on documents, rather than actual collaboration. Thus, teachers may need to consider naming conventions when uploading. For example, making sure the filename has a date stamp and initials (presentation08Oct_js.pptx).

Passwords

Passwords are the bane of everyone's existence. In today's cloud-based, interconnected world, both work and home life revolve around access to social media, banking, work and email sites. We all know that we should have different passwords for every account, and they should be complex (what individuals who work in IT call 'strong' passwords). One is generally advised not to write passwords down, or remain logged in on any computer that could be accessed easily by another person.

There are lots of strategies for creating passwords, and many of them are poor. At the other extreme, password management applications will, for a fee, securely house all of your passwords and automatically login with your credentials with one master password. Having to log in consistently to an account also forces you to remember the password, as opposed to sites where you log in occasionally. However, many tech professionals do not follow their own advice, which I believe paints a clear picture of the difficulties in staying ahead of those who wish to hack into our personal lives.

I generally think about levels of necessary security. There are some things that hackers want to get to, some things they do not, and there is also the consideration of consequences. Someone getting into my bank account is much more serious than someone hacking my Twitter feed. Unless you have 100,000 followers on Twitter, getting hacked is probably more of an annoyance than something that will ruin your credit rating. Here is some advice for various levels of password security:

Financials

- Strong Password (upper and lowercase, numbers, symbols, not a word)
- 2-step authentication (additional security questions and/or a code sent by text or email)
- Do not write down your password

Work accounts

- Strong Password and login (if possible)
- Memorable (you can get away with a word or phrase)
- Do not write down your password at work

Personal email and social media

- Probably can get away with an easy-to-remember password for social media, but not email
- Memorable
- Can write it down at home and keep in a safe place

Rarely accessed (insurance, utility websites, etc.)

- One of your stock passwords
- Memorable
- Write it down and keep in a safe place

A few notes about creating passwords. First, to make them stronger, you must include symbols. You can remember this by using symbols to represent letters, such as @ for a, ! or 1 for L or I, etc. Also, stay away from words, opting more for initials from phrases (e.g., "an apple a day keeps the doctor away, becomes A@aDKt$a). You can also shift your fingers on the keyboard left or right (e.g., "harmony" becomes "jst<pmu"). With respect to writing passwords down, don't write the actual password down. Let's say the "harmony" example was used for your bank. On a saved bank statement, write something like "song left" to give a hint, or if you have a password that you've used for some time but have altered it, write something like "u$ual" to remind yourself that it's one of your 'regulars' that you've strengthened.

Distractions

We live in a world of constant distraction. The myth of the efficient multitasker has been thoroughly debunked. Time split between tasks leads to none of the tasks being completed to the best of our ability. Unfortunately, our ability to focus on one thing at a time is constantly hampered by the plethora of distractions, especially online. Case in point: as we rely more heavily on internet access to complete our work, we are more often able to surf the internet for email, entertainment, and other purposes. I began writing this book on a Google Document, but when I needed to get serious about finishing and editing, I downloaded the files as MS Word documents and went to places where I did not have Wi-Fi access in order to avoid distractions.

There are more practical ways to fight distractions. Lockdown browsers and browser extensions limit your ability to stray from your intended task by preventing access to problematic sites. For example, if you find yourself going to Facebook too often, these add-ons can block the site completely, or allow you to access it for a limited time, say 30 total minutes a day. Once that limit is hit, you can no longer access the site. Alternately, you can create or generate a completely random password for these accounts, write them down, put the password in an inconvenient location, and log off. That way, you must exert a bit of effort to access some sites, which usually defeats the distraction urge. Finally, if you are fortunate enough to have multiple computers or devices, keep yourself logged into these accounts on one computer, but not the other. In other words, have a 'work' device and a 'play' device. When you need to focus, leave the 'play' device in another room, or don't take it with you to the library, coffee shop, or wherever your work location may be.

Conclusions

In the end, this chapter intentionally does not focus on specific tools to use. That is because every school is different, and tools come and go. The primary goal of this chapter is to help promote technology as something that makes life easier rather than more difficult, after some initial up front work. Depending on the school culture, this can have a gateway effect; by making teachers' lives easier through technology, teachers may start thinking about how to use technology to make students' lives easier through better instruction and higher achievement.

Activities

Productivity professional development is multi-faceted, but the primary goal is to have teachers appreciate that, in the long run, technology can help solve the problem of limited time. The initial step is to do a needs assessment, by gauging the needs of the district as well as the needs of the teachers. A technology committee should look across the district and develop training programs for common applications (gradebook, office productivity suite, school website program, etc.). For teachers, an end-of-year survey about problems with technology or a wish list (i.e., "I wish I could use technology to…") should help prioritize the PD agenda for the upcoming school year. For example, if teachers are complaining more about the gradebook than the website software, the gradebook should be a priority. Doing too much on too many different topics will likely lead to confusion and disengagement rather than adoption.

The top 1-3 problems or wish list items should be the key items for the upcoming school year. The technology committee should begin developing a range of activities and job aids for these priorities. Key questions to ask are:

- Will these require group interactions to encourage use and dis-

cussion?
- Can these issues be solved with a simple job aid, such as a laminated sheet at each station?
- Should we create how-to videos in addition to the PD sessions?
- Do we know if these applications are going through an update anytime soon (i.e., thus rendering the job aids and how-to videos dated or obsolete)?
- Do these require a lot of up front work? If so, how/when will this time be provided?
- How can we schedule the PD and other activities to best align with teachers needs (e.g., teachers need to know how to best enter scores into the gradebook right away, but will not need training on submitting final grades until later; setting up a website requires some early help, with job aids shortly after, and follow up PD for advanced features during the middle of the year)?

Performance Improvement without Training

A common misconception in the workplace, particularly in education, is that every problem can be solved with instruction. In other words, there is an automatic assumption that if workers are not performing to the employer's standard, it is because the workers do not know how. In many cases, the workers are intellectually capable and have the knowledge, but they simply fail to perform the required tasks for a host of other reasons. The following reasons are based off Gilbert's (2007) Behavior Engineering Model.

Information

While training can increase a teacher's capabilities for using technology, perhaps a lack of access to data or other information prevents the teacher from utilizing either technology or specific instructional strategies. For example, if a teachers want to differentiate their instruction, they need access to student data such as test scores and IEP information. Without getting into a discussion on FERPA (although student data use for improving the instructional process should be an acceptable reason for access), individualizing instruction to a particular student requires knowledge of things such as the student's reading level. If teachers have insufficient data on their students, they cannot successfully differentiate their instruction, even if they're well versed in the concept.

Resources

Perhaps teachers do not integrate technology into their instruction because the technology they have access to is outdated. Or perhaps the access to technology is limited, in the case of a large high school with only one or two computer labs. Internet bandwidth might also be low, and teachers become frustrated when they bring a classroom of students to the lab, and can get nothing done (which leads to unwanted distractions and disruptions). Resources are often scarce in education; however, my point here is to illustrate that the best professional development will not overcome these hurdles.

Capacity

Teachers may have the knowledge and skills, but, as mentioned earlier, lack the time to implement said skills. Instead of administration investing time in training, perhaps they should examine how they can help free up time for teachers, or create an environment that facilitates creativity and collaboration. Is there the potential to give teachers common planning time within a department or grade level? What about delayed start times or early release times for students? How could these be formalized, and how can members of the administration win community support, given that public education often means affordable day care for working parents, and any disruption will invite cynicism and scrutiny? Can other training be moved to online modules, with a requirement that teachers complete them at their convenience, using the freed up time for working with colleagues? Can procedural training be competency based, meaning that teachers can skip required training if they can demonstrate competency in the area for which the mandatory training is given?

Incentives

While we eschew extrinsic motivation for the "love of learning" within our classrooms, as adults we also realize that incentives can lead to desired behaviors. Obviously, monetary incentives would be nice, but next to impossible to provide in the educational context. Further, merit pay for student performance is difficult to measure (value-add models are shaky at best) and also invite deception in one way or another. So, what are some perks that could be offered to teachers? Every school and district is unique, but extra time and preferential treatment for resources are two possible rewards.

Giving teachers the opportunity to work from home, for example is a great incentive. If a teacher demonstrates competency with the online gradebook, that teacher might be allowed to stay home for records day when the students are not there. Using the example from the previous section, if teachers complete online PD, they can stay home for some of that time. However, with the previous example, completing online PD allowed for collaboration time, that freed up time was for working with colleagues; implementers must be careful to not mix the two.

Preferential treatment sounds a bit unprofessional at first, but by requiring teachers to demonstrate competency before accessing resources makes plenty of sense. Let's say you want to encourage teachers to use technology in ways other than researching online in the computer lab, assembling PowerPoint presentations, or typing papers. Provide resources and training on transformative technology use, and give teachers who demonstrate some competency with integrating technology with high leverage instructional strategies preferential access to computer labs.

Motives

Most teachers simply want to "shut their door and teach." So, why would they take the time to learn something that they may or may not use, that requires some initial effort to set things up? Circling back to adult learning theory, teachers need to see the benefits firsthand. Before providing training to a wide audience of teachers, it is necessary to focus on the early adopters or the pioneers, and use them as "living proof" for why more skeptical teachers should spend extra time with training and practicing.

More importantly, many teachers have been through cycle after cycle of poorly developed professional development. They may not buy in simply because they don't want to get burned again by a one-time PD session that falls flat or an initiative with no follow through. Thus, building trust with teachers and being able to demonstrate both value and commitment before any training takes place is the key to motivating teachers.

References

Gilbert, T.F. (2007). *Human competence: Engineering worthy performance.* San Francisco, CA: Pfeiffer.
Hattie, J. (2008). *Visible learning: A synthesis of over 800 meta-analyses relating to achievement.* New York: Routledge.
Knowles, M. S., Holton III, E. F., & Swanson, R. A. (2005). *The adult learner: The definitive classic in adult education and human resource development (6th ed.).* Burlington, MA: Elsevier.

Chapter 3

Preferment

When I was working on this model of technology integration, this "P" was the hardest to define and develop. When discussing the matter with colleagues, many suggested I use the word "promotion" instead. However, I did not feel that the term was appropriate, because it smacked of notions that I abhor in educational technology: merely promoting technology in classrooms for the sake of technology. Further, promotion is not the best term when discussing issues that negatively affect technology integration in classrooms, namely issues concerning access and cultural bias.

Therefore, I settled on the term preferment, which means "advancement." This chapter deals with issues and trends in technology that affect, either positively or negatively, teachers' ability to use technology in the classroom for instruction. This is more of a critical view of technology in the classroom; that is, for every good use of technology, there are unintended consequences, and for every drawback associated with technology, there are opportunities for learning and discussion.

The Digital Divide

The Digital Divide is probably the most prominent issue in K-12 technology integration. Simply put, it is the fact that schools have varying levels of resources; some have a lot of technology at their disposal, and some do not. Zooming in a bit more, we also know that students come from different socioeconomic backgrounds, and therefore have varying levels of technology at home.

Unfortunately, in the 21st Century we have begun to make assumptions about this generation of students. We are led to believe that they are "digital natives" since they have grown up in a world where they are surrounded by technology, they act and think differently, they are adept at using technology, and they "understand" its potential far more than those from previous generations, who grew up in a world before the internet, mobile devices, and so on.

All of these assumptions could be true, but the anchor of the assumption is that children from this generation a) have these devices at their disposal, and b) have had the guidance from their parents or guardians on how to use them to leverage educational and economic advantage. As you read these sentences, think about the student population that your school serves. Is that a solid assumption for every single student?

For some readers, the answer is yes. For some, the answer is no. Likely, though, the answer lies somewhere in the middle. This can handcuff teachers trying to effectively integrate technology in the classroom. What is more troubling is how this has limited technology's effectiveness in increasing student achievement. Why? Because if you teach in a district that does not give every student a device, even if the school has adequate technology, home access is key. Therefore, educators are faced with a choice. They water down the technology use to the level where they are simply replacing traditional methods with technology (with little or no added functionality), or they use technology in high leverage ways realizing that some students will be unable to realize some (or all) of the effects because they lack access outside of the classroom.

While the implications of such inequities is tremendous when you consider national disparities, the purpose of this book is to address the varying needs to students within your particular district or building. Thus, professional development on the topic of inequities of access must be addressed as part of a larger professional development session on technology.

At this point, the access issue often boils down to a reactionary argument about how students can come before or after school, or at lunch time or recess, to access the computer labs. Further down this black hole are nostalgic arguments about having to go to the library because the home lacked encyclopedias or particular books. However, these arguments simply pass the blame on to external factors, thus excusing the teacher from any blame for a student's lack of achievement.

For example, consider the suggested alternative time for using a computer lab. This, of course, first assumes that a computer lab is open during these times, or that teachers are consistently available in their classrooms to allow students to use technology. Second, it assumes that the students have transportation options to get to school early or stay later. Alternately, it assumes that, for the morning option, the buses arrive to give them enough time. Again, are these assumptions valid for a poor student? Do they have cars? Can a parent alter their work schedule to transport them? Do the bus routes that serve the low income housing arrive well before the morning bell? Now, consider lunch time. First, does the school allow food outside the cafeteria? Second, since poor students often receive free or reduced lunch, do they have time to get in line, get lunch, eat lunch, leave the cafeteria, and go do work? Remember, "just bring a lunch from home that day," may not be an option.

In short, these barriers, along with a possible lack of knowledge on effective technology integration (addressed in other chapters) often lead to teachers either not using technology at all, or using it in such a superficial way that academic gains are minimal, if any, when compared to a more traditional instructional approach that does not utilize technology.

So, why use technology in the first place? The evidence regarding technology use in the classroom and its effect on achievement is mixed. Some studies show benefits, others show no significant change, some show the effects wearing off over time (novelty wears off), and some show the pitfalls of technology. While in the pedagogy chapter we will cover the achievement issue, there are reasons unrelated to achievement.

Think back to your classes on sociology, philosophy, and anthropology. Over the course of human history, power has come in the form of controlling the means of production. For example, in an agrarian society, the owners of the land had all of the wealth, because they controlled the primary asset in wealth creation... land on which crops were grown. In an industrial society, the factory owners controlled the wealth. In the information age in which we currently live, it is those who have the knowledge and skills to create the hardware and software that are amassing wealth.

But this discussion is much more than about wealth. Sure, those students who have exposure to technology and a good education will likely find themselves with a good job in the future. However, the other aspect of controlling the means of production is the ability to have a say in cultural norms. Certain aspects of our culture are present due to the cultural values installed during the agrarian, industrial, and information ages. During the industrial age, mass educational practices mirrored the need for a consistent and obedient factory worker. In the agrarian society, access to education was limited to the wealthy and the pious; again, keeping the farmer near subsistence but obedient to the divinely anointed royalty.

Cultural values can run along both race and gender. If the current technology environment is dominated by white males, guess what? The values of white males end up in the technology. Computer code is culturally neutral, just like a letter of the alphabet. However, as the alphabet can be used to form words, sentences, and thoughts, computer code can be written to create products that reflect perceived needs, desires, and values of their creators. Want to create a false image of beauty? Create a program that can alter images! Want to distract people with mindless entertainment? Create simplistic yet addictive games, or short pieces of faux journalism highlighting pointless bits of information!

Thus, it is not enough to simply teach students how to use technology. Many of them already know how, and many can probably operate devices better than the teacher in the classroom. However, just plunking down laptops or tablets in the hands of every student in the room does not increase academic achievement nor does it create tech wizards of the future. The problem is that we often mistake consumption for production. We give students devices, provide them with assignments that are basically no different from the assignments we gave them before said devices existed, and wonder a) why achievement has not increased (if it's measured at all, that is...more on this elsewhere in the book), or b) why interest in technology careers still wanes. More importantly, teachers and parents express discontent when students simply use the devices for gaming and social media, i.e., doing the things they were told not to do given this "opportunity."

These behaviors occur because we are doing too little to encourage the shift from consumers of technology to producers of technology and media. In the following sections, I take a critical view of several current trends in K-12 educational technology. I think that all of these trends can be beneficial to student learning and in helping to close the digital divide… if done correctly.

1:1/BYOD

One of the problems with this phenomenon is that districts are currently trying to "keep up with the Joneses" by moving to a system called 1:1, where each student is provided with a mobile device, such as a tablet, or a laptop. A similar system is called BYOD, or Bring Your Own Device. Districts sell this idea to the community, and, in the case of 1:1, they must literally sell this idea in the form of voting on a bond or millage. Some win, some lose. For the winners, the devices arrive with much pomp and circumstance, and magically the students end up learning something, but not necessarily more than they would have before the devices arrived.

The secret sauce here is professional development. Did the teachers receive adequate training in the technical aspects of the devices (how to use them) and the procedural aspects (how to manage a class with them)? The answer is pretty likely. However, did the teachers receive any pedagogical training; how to use the devices in the context of their content and grade specific best practices and teaching methods, demonstrating ways in which they could use the devices for evidence-based instructional practices that were previously impractical or impossible without the technology? The answer is likely not.

The reason why the answer is negative is that who in the district is a pedagogical expert in every grade and subject? Who is also skilled in technology and pedagogy? Further, teachers are likely to believe that they are the experts in their own domain, which may lead to a bit of resistance when someone (a peer, and outsider, basically anyone who is not an education professor, which may be even more ridiculous) tries to tell them how to teach.

To overcome these negative feelings, the professional development should be structured in a way to address these concerns. First, assuaging those negative feelings should begin with professional development demonstrating how the technology can be beneficial to the teacher (i.e., the professionalism and productivity chapters). Next, the professional development should focus on the technical skills necessary to operate the device, followed by the management aspect. In other words, the educators should be comfortable with using the devices, in addition to being able to use them for their own personal benefit. Then, the talk can turn to pedagogy.

Distance Education

Distance education has increased tremendously in the K-12 sector. However, training to teach in the medium, where students may never physically interact with their instructor, has lagged. In my experiences, many pre-service teachers I work with are somewhat dismissive of online education as a career, even in part. Many of them say they went into teaching for purpose of interacting with children, and they believe that online education does not satisfy their requirement.

The other issue with online education is that its effectiveness (and yes, it is just as effective as traditional instruction, when done right) is often overshadowed by the political and economic baggage that often accompanies online initiatives. Some feel that it is less about educating students with unique considerations and more about the competition for students (and the dollars they bring with them when they leave another district to take your classes).

Further, some of these mandates are done under the guise of preparing students for online learning in the "real world" and even the dreaded "21st Century skills" moniker, when in reality it may be about cutting overhead, either classroom space or staffing requirements.

In short, however, online education does serve the purpose of providing education to students under special circumstances (gifted students working ahead, credit recovery, access for homebound students, students in small districts who want classes that simply cannot be offered, students who must work, etc.). Professional development in this area should revolve around the instructor capabilities as well as how to properly act as a course facilitator, since many courses are not provided in house, but rather through a third-party vendor.

On a larger scale, professional development should educate teachers on the merits and pitfalls of the medium. It is not a panacea for all that ails public education, and a district staff should be well informed of these issues. Further, the district and its teachers should be in agreement (as much as labor and management can agree) about the scope and purpose of the distance education offerings. Further, labor and management need to agree upon the responsibilities of both sides when it comes to working conditions and compensation, as online courses are indeed different in scope and workload.

Blended Learning

A more likely trend in schools is the push toward blended learning, where at least some of the physical face-to-face time is replaced with online learning. This does not mean that students are given extra online work; that falls more under the umbrella of web-enhanced instruction. In blended models, face-to-face time is replaced; that is, students likely do not come to class everyday. Obviously, this brings up concerns of monitoring students, transportation, and safety.

Like with online learning, there needs to be a solid reason for doing so. Again, is the primary purpose for exposure to the medium, or are there other reasons for going through the scheduling and transportation nightmare to improve student outcomes?

With respect to professional development, blended learning is different from face-to-face and online learning. Designing a blended course requires much more thought in determining not only logistics, but determining what course content can be done online and what should or must be done in class. Further, design decisions in daily lesson planning should take into account what content can be done at a student's own pace and what is required to be completed before a face-to-face session.

Flipped Learning

A more recent trend is the "flipped" classroom. The concept of 'flipping' a classroom implies that the direct instruction, usually conducted by the teacher in class, is now provided online. Conversely, the work that was normally done at home is now done in class, allowing for teachers to provide immediate help and assistance, instead of students having problems doing the work at home and either not completing the homework, not understanding, and not being able to get just-in-time assistance.

In theory, this sounds so intuitive, it makes one wonder why we have not picked up on this a long time ago. However, the concept has been around for quite some time. How many college courses assumed that you had done the readings before coming to class? Isn't that what teachers meant by "being prepared"?

Therein lies the initial problem with a flipped classroom. If you told students to read something before coming to class the next day, how much compliance do you expect? Further, do you expect that compliance to skyrocket once you tell them to watch video lectures instead? Therefore, professional development in this area should revolve around both purpose and structure. Flipping a classroom is more than just posting lecture videos online and students doing problem sets in class. PD should involve how to ensure that students take the first encounter with content seriously without being punitive, how to make sure that those first encounters are necessary (e.g., if a teacher reviews the online lecture in class, why would a student watch it?), and what types of activities and class setups ensure that learning is differentiated so that students of all capabilities are engaged during the class time (e.g., what to do about students who understand quickly, rather than give them extra problems they do not need, etc.).

Coding

The buzz these days in technology education is coding. Referring back to what was mentioned earlier about owning the means of production, there has been a push to teach students how to write code in a variety of programming languages. In the past, coding was very complex and difficult to teach to young students. However, there are several languages available to students created to maintain the same nuances of computational thinking, but have a simple user interface to allow very young children to participate. Further, several services exist on the internet geared toward teaching common programming languages to children and adults alike packaged in small, digestible modules that allow for self-paced learning.

One of the major issues with coding is the disconnect to content. Many coding initiatives are limited to enrichment activities, occurring before school, after school (remember the transportation concerns?), at lunch (likewise), or during a school-wide event such as the National Hour of Code. For this phenomenon to mean something (i.e., meet its intended purpose of teaching code more than just a novelty event as well as encouraging students, particularly females and minorities, to pursue careers in computer science), it needs to be fully integrated into core curriculum.

The benefit of these coding languages is that they are indeed easy to learn, which means that teachers can learn them as well without being computer science majors themselves. Professional development in this area should revolve around teaching teachers how to code, as well as planning time to develop lessons that involve coding. Further, a vertical alignment of the curriculum should explore how both grade levels and subject areas use coding to teach or create projects, keeping in mind that there's more to programming than just knowing code. Some of those fundamentals (e.g., storyboarding, debugging) can be taught without computers, and basic skills could be taught in isolation in a technology pull out class or within specific grades and subjects.

Digital Citizenship

Digital citizenship is a broad term that covers how students (and teachers, for that matter) act in a digital environment. It can range from simply online etiquette to code switching (i.e., how texting your friends requires a different set of rules and standards than writing an email to your teachers or professor) to protecting one's identity to cyberbullying. Also, since we live in a world where more and more intellectual property is in a digital format (music, books, etc.) concepts of copyright and fair use (in the case of the latter, more for teachers) also fall under the umbrella of digital citizenship.

Age appropriateness is always a concern when discussing the aforementioned issues. "How young is too young?" is a question and concern with certain topics such as sexting (i.e., sending lewd photos via text messages), but also for more practical concerns, such as teaching very young children about credit card theft.

Making the issues even more murky are those unrelated to professional development. Some of these topics are disciplinary, even criminal in nature. Because of the nature of digital communication, it is not always clear on where a school's jurisdiction ends. Does these mean that we should not engage the students in discussion of these topics? Of course not! Professional development on this topic should focus on educating teachers on the various rules and laws, the school's Acceptable Use Policy (AUP), how to discuss these issues with students, and vertically aligning a digital citizenship curriculum to prevent "passing the buck" (i.e., pushing the curriculum to the lower grades to limit responsibility).

Activities

Perhaps the most important activity that must be done to advance technology with your learners is to conduct a learner analysis for the building and explicitly share this information with your staff. Most of this data is already known to central office and the administrative staff. It is a matter of collecting it and sharing it with teachers as a starting point to understanding the learners and what they bring to the table: good, bad, and ugly. It is also noteworthy because it can show the differences and gaps between the different demographics. Once teachers are made aware of these differences, a discussion can arise on how the school can meet the needs of these students, as well as brainstorm ideas for ensuring access and equity.

From a building or district standpoint, horizontal and vertical alignment of technology expectations needs to occur. In other words, what can a teacher reasonably expect students to do based on what they have learned in previous years? Care must be taken to ensure that the lower grades are not excessively tasked with teaching everything, so that the higher grade levels can focus on their content. This is particularly challenging at the high school level, where students have a more differentiated course schedule. In this case, care must be taken not to excessively burden the common courses that every student in a particular grade must take.

If your school or district wants to emphasize computational thinking and coding skills, embedding it into the core curriculum, this vertical alignment process must take place. It can be a combination of actual programming, computational skills, and design; however, the earlier the students are exposed to writing code, the better. For example, the International Society for Technology in Education states that computation thinking involves the following skills:

- Formulating problems in a way that enables us to use a computer and other tools to help solve them.
- Logically organizing and analyzing data
- Representing data through abstractions such as models and simulations
- Automating solutions through algorithmic thinking (a series of ordered steps)
- Identifying, analyzing, and implementing possible solutions with the goal of achieving the most efficient and effective combinations of steps and resources
- Generalizing and transferring this problem solving process to a wide variety of problems (ISTE, 2011, para. 2)

As you can see, actual programming and coding is rarely mentioned in these processes. Further, many teachers inject these skills and ideas into their instructional already. As I mentioned earlier, very few K-12 teachers have experience in programming; however, they have experience with the computational thinking skillset. What is missing, again, is the vertical alignment of these skills across grade levels, with computer science and programming opportunities woven throughout. Programming languages have become incredibly intuitive and easy for young children to learn, but along with these experiences, the associated thinking skills also need to be integrated into the curriculum. Finally, as with any well planned technology initiative, long-term goals should be created and progress toward those goals should be monitored. After aligning curriculum and experiences across several grades and levels, data from the following sources should be monitored:

- Interest surveys from students
- Surveys from teachers on comfort levels teaching programming and related skills
- Participation in programming/coding enrichment activities (early and middle grades)
- Test scores
- Enrolments in computer science classes (middle and high school)
- College readiness scores
- Career intentions
- College degree completions

In closing, we are currently faced with the challenge of proving technology's worth in K-12 schools. So far, we have failed to provide sufficient evidence, and this lack of progress with technology comes at the taxpayer's expense. We are also facing a challenge of closing an equity gap with our students when it comes to technology. While much of this is related to equity in funding in schools across the country, it is also about understanding how technology relates to power in society. Unless we have a concerted effort to provide opportunities for all of our students to move from consumers of technology to producers of technology, the gap between the haves and have-nots will continue to grow. In order to address this divide, we must close the technology gap between those who "do" technology and those who "can't."

References

International Society for Technology in Education (2011). *Operational Definition of Computational Thinking for K-12 Education*. Retrieved from http://www.iste.org/docs/ct-documents/computational-thinking-operational-definition-flyer.pdf?sfvrsn=2

Chapter 4

Pedagogy

This chapter is arguably the toughest one to write, and it is also the toughest form of professional development to implement. Why? Because pedagogy can be so specific, both with respect to content area and grade level. Further, those in charge of creating and implementing professional development on pedagogy may be far removed from the classroom for many years. In addition, even if they are current classroom teachers, they may only have a small perspective of this whole range of pedagogies. In my own experiences as a secondary science teacher, I have a narrow view of good pedagogy for my age range and content. In other words, I do not know best practices and strategies for elementary students, or in subjects other than science.

Adding to this issue is the skepticism teachers may own because of these facts. "The principal, a former elementary teacher with an ELA certification that has not been in front of students in 20 years, is going to tell me how to teach physics? Please…," will likely be uttered in some similar form by more than a few teachers. Therefore, it may be better to approach this from a departmental standpoint. In other words, let the experts be the experts. However, there is some general discussion of instructional strategies that can occur. More importantly, and with regards to technology, the staff should begin to question the use of technology. That's right, question the use of technology.

One of the definitions of technology is the application of human knowledge to solve problems. Do we have problems in education? Most definitely! Does every teacher have a problem with student outcomes at some point during the year? Of course (and if they claim not to, well, they are either a rock star teacher, lack any awareness of their student needs, or are simply satisfied with the status quo). Therefore, the approach with technology should be to solve some problem associated with learning outcomes.

While the preferment chapter discussed the need for a learner analysis to truly understand a school's diversity, teachers should look at the needs and goals of each class. Perhaps the teachers need to look at the outcomes for the class. Not the standards, the outcomes. Many teachers, myself included at some point, have not really sat down and verbalized or written down what we want our students to know, understand, etc., when they finish a lesson, unit, or course. Some of that is due to the fact that a lot of curriculum is pre-fabricated through either a textbook (and all of their ancillary materials, worksheets, test banks, etc.) and through state and/or national standards.

The problem is that standards and objectives from these sources are somewhat vague and general in nature. As educators, we want to have something attainable and measurable, not the usual "students will know…" that is often found on standards and the outcomes listed at the beginning of a textbook chapter. Thus, some PD time should be spent on objective writing or on learning outcomes. Once these goals are decided, then the staff can proceed to work on best instructional strategies for achieving these goals.

Alternatively, these goals could be approached on a school-wide level, avoiding the specificity of content areas. Let's say that your school as a whole scores low in reading comprehension. Well, there's your problem. What types of instructional strategies can the entire staff learn and implement, and how can technology assist in implementing those strategies, collecting data when those strategies are employed, and analyzing the data to determine whether the strategies worked?

"Worked" is a loaded term, unless goals have been set BEFORE the implementation of any initiative begins. If goals are met or exceeded, then the strategy worked. However, if no goals or benchmarks are set, it is very easy to say something "worked." Why? First, confirmation bias plays a huge role. That is, unless a teacher is collecting data, it becomes easy to believe that something worked based on anecdotes and emotion. The amount of work a teacher put into something new influences the belief of improved outcomes. Second, and more problematic, is that in education, everything works.

The "Everything Works" Problem

Hattie's (2008) research on effect sizes related to teaching and learning found that there are few, if any, instructional strategies that negatively impact learning. His findings should make sense; unless teachers are blatantly misinforming students, there is little an educator can do to make a child less smart. While this fact does not sound like a problem, we need to begin to address the fact that we need to move beyond this fact and work toward using the tools and strategies that work best.

In a previous age—the Industrial age currently winding down—students in schools were primarily educated to be productive members of the workforce. The majority of these students were headed to manufacturing and skilled labor jobs primarily requiring specialized skills in a certain area. Most of the knowledge for these jobs was obtained through apprenticeships and the like, and knowledge in academic subjects was, for the most part, not required. Further, a student could graduate from high school and head straight into the workforce with a job on the assembly line. When I say "graduate", I mean that students could do the bare minimum and learn basic skills to earn a diploma, then go on to a job through which a middle-class lifestyle could be obtained. Thus, the fact that everything worked, even just a little, was sufficient in education.

Today, things are different. Generally speaking, students can no longer attain a comfortable middle-class lifestyle through a job obtained right after high school. Sure, there are exceptions, and those who pursue profitable interests outside of school are more the exception than the norm. Simply put, service jobs do not pay as well as manufacturing or skilled labor jobs, and most people with only a high school education are qualified for little more than jobs in the service sector. This means that students need to be successful during their K-12 years in order to progress through various post-secondary avenues, if they wish to have any chance of self-sufficiency. In addition, even just navigating through our increasingly advanced world requires more than just basic knowledge. Navigating through the world of savings and finance, law, medicine, or even dealing with your car or computers can be incredibly confusing unless you have some basic to intermediate literacy in these areas. The alternative of just trusting the experts without question can leave one vulnerable.

We are also living in a time of information overload. In the past, there were a few trusted sources of information that we could rely on for relatively unbiased news and commentary. Today, we must vet each and every source, researching the research to follow a money trail. While I am not a fan of the term "21st Century Skills" (i.e., an amalgamation of critical thinking, problem solving, and information literacy skills whose name implies that said skills weren't necessary during the previous 20 centuries), students as well as adults need to be critical consumers of information now more than ever, and this takes more than just telling students not to believe everything they read on the internet.

Then, for the sake of this book, we need to look at how technology can enhance or enable those best practices…to achieve the stated learning outcomes. However, we should first return to the issue of goal setting and outcomes, as this is the foundation for making sure that educators pinpoint problems, paint a picture of success, and collect data to measure progress toward that picture.

From Standards to Outcomes

Since Common Core State Standards (CCSS) are copyrighted, I will use different standards as examples in this section. Let's begin with a few social studies standards from the Michigan Merit Curriculum (see https://www.michigan.gov/documents/mde/SS_HSCE_9-15-09_292358_7.pdf):

- *K1.3 Understand and analyze social relationships and patterns*
- *1.1.3 Identify and explain competing arguments about the necessity and purposes of government (such as to protect inalienable rights, promote the general welfare, resolve conflicts, promote equality, and establish justice for all)*

While the first standard is under the heading of "General Skills," it is clear that there is no practical way for a teacher or student to demonstrate some proficiency in this standard without some modification and interpretation. A red flag should appear any time a standard or objective contains the words *know* or *understand*, as there is no tangible way to see this in children without coming up with your own determination of how a student would successfully demonstrate their knowledge. The second standard provides two tangible verbs—identify and explain—which is better, but the standard provides no indication of quality of the explanation. Again, this is left for the educator to determine. Again, I am not criticizing the standards; I am simply stating my opinion that the educator needs to interpret these standards in a way that is measurable and makes sense to not only the teacher but to a student as well.

Translating standards to actions that can be measured can be done in a variety of ways. The simplest way is to write behavioral objectives. These typically involve translating a standard into a short sentence containing the following elements: audience, behavior, condition, and degree, or ABCD for easy reference. The audience portion is your typical, "Learners will..." introductory phrase. The key to the behavior is that is should be an actionable verb that can be observed (i.e., not "know" or "understand"). The conditions may be some limiting factors or situations under which the performance should occur. Finally, the degree is to what level or extent the behavior must be repeated or to what level of accuracy it must be performed. Examples include:

- Students will perform 2-step stoichiometric calculations with 80% accuracy.
- The learner will state and provide an example of each of the 3 phases of matter.
- Students will write an expository essay that earns a rating of proficient or higher on 4 of the 5 criteria on the rubric.

These allow teachers to verbalize what they believe is sufficient performance for a student to have mastered a specific content standard. Further, these also serve as concise statements for students to understand what is expected of them. Finally, since they are measurable, teachers can collect quantifiable data as a way to track progress or compare methods and strategies to see what works "best."

A similar technique involves creating a range of demonstrable competencies that can also be quantified. It usually involves four distinct and measurable levels, with proficiency being at the third level. These can be called learning targets, outcomes, "I can..." statements, and a few others. Taking the first objective from the previous example, a continuum might look like this:

- Level 1: The learner cannot complete a 2-step stoichiometric calculation.
- Level 2: The learner can complete a 2-step stoichiometric calculation with assistance.
- Level 3: The learner can complete 2-step stoichiometric calculations without assistance with at least 80% accuracy.
- Level 4: The learner can complete 2-step and 3-step stoichiometric calculations without assistance with at least 80% accuracy.

Using this method, teachers can collect data on how students progress. While this is ordinal data (i.e., using numbers 1-4), at least some minor descriptive statistics can be used to show progress throughout a unit or when comparing whether a new strategy showed increases in student outcomes.

Pioneers, Skeptics, and Cynics

In any organization, you have those who lead the way, some who need some convincing, and some who will never be convinced: the pioneers, the skeptics, and they cynics. The largest and most important group in determining the success of a PD initiative are the skeptics. Skeptics have been burned too many times to simply buy into whatever is presented as a way to help students succeed, particularly if they have invested time and energy into previous initiatives that were unsuccessful or abandoned prematurely. By promoting efforts to make their lives easier, (i.e., the topics and skills from the Professionalism and Productivity chapters), should help in convincing the skeptics to be willing participants.

Another way to encourage the buy in from reluctant staff is to play to their strengths. The reason this can be easy and effective is that what many teachers do is indeed effective, and it usually has a track record of research behind it. This can help to persuade these reluctant staff that the district is not simply jumping on the next hottest fad or buying technology for the sake of looking good, but rather because they are using research to inform their decision.

The administration needs to be cautious, however, when using research to inform their practice for two reasons. First, as mentioned previously, just about everything we do in education works to some extent. Second, administration must not simply cherry pick studies that suit their needs. Given the recent issues with scientific reproducibility (studies that try to replicate results in related areas such as psychology often cannot do so), picking a single study on which to base their efforts will likely lead to little change in student performance.

Thus, administrators should look to research such as literature reviews and meta-analyses, studies that aggregate the results of many different studies to draw general conclusions, to drive pedagogy and technology PD. Once these high leverage strategies are identified, then PD can focus on how technology can make these strategies possible, easier to implement, and how to institutionalize them.

This should not mean that every new trend in education should be dismissed. However, the adoption of new pedagogies should be more careful and thoughtful than reading the latest issue of an educational magazine or a blog post from a professional speaker. These ideas and topics should be discussed (as they will have been made known through the PLNs of teachers and administrators) as possible changes in the future. Further, these ideas could be piloted in small areas of the district (including data collection, analysis, and possible publication of the results), rather than a large-scale adoption.

The Role of Technology

When it comes to technology, there are several ways to think about integration. However, the main point is what does it bring to the table that could not be done before it. Think about it this way. There have been great teachers in the history of education well before Steve Jobs plunked down an Apple II in a classroom back in the 1980's. The other thing to think about is backup plans. For example, when the internet is down or the lab is double-booked. If those backup plans essentially accomplish the same goal, then why bother with the technology in the first place? Finally, think about the latest buzz in technology. A few years ago, Prezi was all the rage for presentations. Kids "liked" them because they were cooler and much more "engaging" than PowerPoints. In hindsight, people probably viewed PowerPoints the same way 20 years ago when they were first being utilized as lecture tools. But then, the novelty wore off. How soon (if not already) will the same occur for Prezi?

The final example in the previous paragraph demonstrates a core principle of technology integration: pedagogy before technology. The difference between using a chalkboard, whiteboard, PowerPoint, or Prezi is basically minimal because the instructional strategy in most cases is the same, lecture and direct instruction. In reality, some of these offer minor benefits, but since the instructional strategy is the same, the results will likely be the same when you apply them. Any 'perk' in the process (e.g., the students seem to enjoy it, act more interested, etc.) will generally be a novelty effect that declines over time or as a result of teacher bias (e.g., "I did something different that took extra time, and I KNOW the kids liked it," when, in reality, it's an illusion created by the teacher to convince them that the effort was worth it).

Contrast the above paragraph with using the same tool for different purposes. PowerPoint was originally intended as business presentation software and was coopted by the K-12 and higher education communities as a means of lecture. It can add some functionality to the lecture process (it can be easier to read, it can embed hyperlinks and videos, you can move back and forth, etc.), but, in essence, it is still lecture.

Over time, teachers found other uses for PowerPoint. For example, students are often tasked with giving group presentations. This was something done before the advent of PowerPoint, with students either presenting without any visuals or by using physical items, such as posters. It does not enhance the collaborative process of group work, and aside from the possible addition of video to the presentation, does little to enhance the group presentation effort. It is an add-on to a research project. Another example is the ever popular review game using PowerPoint, which is set up similar to the TV show Jeopardy. Review questions are created within the presentation, with a first slide that has hyperlinks to each of the questions. Aside from some novelty factor, these are no different than a review worksheet, and this can also be done with a whiteboard (with markers only), with questions being read off a separate sheet of paper (conversely, the questions can be made on paper that is laminated along with some magnetic tape to recreate the TV game board). In terms of strategy, it is similar to review or drill and practice with flash cards. Some gamifying elements have been added, but in a class of 30 put into teams, participation is often limited to a few people; thus, any motivating effects from the gamification are limited to those few, while the others disengage.

So far, none of these uses of PowerPoint seem really all that different from strategies that, for the most part, can be easily accomplished using non-technological means. As a contrast, my dissertation research involved the use of PowerPoint as a tool to design (rather than simply play) games. Students worked in teams to create a game about the topic of study. The game creation process, dubbed constructionism by educational researcher Seymour Papert as students learned by building a specific artifact, contained several evidence-based instructional strategies. First, students needed to write their own questions for the game. Question-writing by students is an instructional strategy that enhances student performance on tests. Second, students needed to write a storyline that embedded elements of fiction with content. Writing-across-the-curriculum strategies are also useful strategies for improving student performance. In addition to the instructional strategies, students practiced elements of computational thinking, a way of thinking as it relates to computer programming. Students had to create games and storylines, arrange and sequence events, and debug the game at the end to check for errors in its construction.

This was a radically different approach to the use of PowerPoint. It was not a presentation, and it was not a teacher-led lecture. One would argue that it is similar to the Jeopardy game, but those are created by the teacher and not the students. Plus, the Jeopardy game is simply review questions, not questions about content centered on a storyline (with characters and plot) created by the students themselves. Could the students create the games using programming software? Yes, but many teachers would not implement such a project due to their lack of programming skills. Because of the pervasive use of PowerPoint in schools, the only additional technique students and teachers often needed to learn was how to add an action button to a slide. Could the games be created without the technology? Yes (and it should be noted that the games created often had external pieces such as game boards, dice, etc.), but the resource use of creating several classes of board games, with pieces, game cards, boxes, etc., would also be a barrier to implementation. (It should also be noted that these games could be created with PowerPoint, Google Slides, and Keynote for Mac users.)

Now, I am not saying that the purpose of PowerPoint in education is solely for the purpose of creating games. Rather, my point was to demonstrate how rather than use different tools for the same instructional strategy, we should be looking first at the pedagogy, THEN looking at the technologies that make it easier or even possible to implement.

Another example would be giving feedback to students. Research has shown (Hattie, 2008) that the keys to feedback making a difference in student learning are the quantity of feedback (more is better), the quality of feedback (specifics, corrective rather than punitive, etc.) and the turnaround time (feedback given on assignments turned in when the class has moved on is less effective). We could also consider the use of peer feedback and teaching here as well.

Using collaborative documents, such as Google Docs, allows students to automatically "submit" their work in the form of a shared document (i.e., shared with the teacher). The teacher can view the document at any time, and write comments directly on the student's paper. They can suggest edits, and can also see if the student has taken those suggestions (via the Revision History feature as well as others). Documents can also be shared with other students, and they can comment on their work as well.

Using online quizzes or computer programs that do drill-and-practice type games, the student receives immediate feedback on their efforts. Depending on the quality of the program, the students may even receive corrective feedback that tells them why their answer was incorrect.

Contrast this with the traditional method of the student handing in an assignment, the teacher taking a stack of papers home, grading them, coming back, and redistributing them. Even if the students submit drafts, there's a specific time for submission, and quite a delay in returning them. In the case of sharing with peers, imagine the mayhem of controlling for lost papers, journals, and so on. Is it possible to give good feedback under these conditions? Yes, it is...we've done it this way for centuries! But, if the goal is meeting the criteria of quality feedback, and we know technology can assist in doing so, shouldn't that be a top priority when designing professional development for teachers?

Justifying Technology

The other key component when tying technology to teaching and learning is being able to justify the use of technology. In order to do so, it is helpful to have some sort of matrix, continuum, or taxonomy of technology use. There is a pitfall with doing so, however. Consider Bloom's taxonomy, regardless of whether you learned the original, revised, or digital version. It is merely a taxonomy of levels of thinking. It should not assume better or worse, good or bad, or even hard or easy (some people would find memorizing Latin verb tenses harder than analyzing poetry). In fact, you could argue that Knowledge (or Remembering) is at the bottom and the largest/widest not because it is the easiest, but because it serves as a foundation for the upper levels. In other words, it is the most important because without it, you cannot to the rest. As any homebuilder knows, if you have a bad foundation, the quality of the work above ground is irrelevant.

Another view of taxonomies in education is to categorize your work to ensure that a teacher is indeed playing in all of the areas of the sandbox of the continuum. A teacher who only teaches rote memorization is no better or worse than a teacher who only claims to teach higher order thinking. The same holds true for the use of technology.

There are many technology integration taxonomies and matrices out there, but I will focus on one, the RAT framework (Hughes et al, 2006). It is very basic in nature. It assumes that technology is used as a replacement for a traditional method or instructional strategy, an amplification of a traditional method (i.e. some increase in features or functionality), or a transformation of a traditional method into something completely different, one that is impossible or difficult to achieve without the use of said technology.

The previous example of using a PowerPoint to present a lecture versus a writing on a whiteboard is a good example of a Replacement activity. Nothing really changes other than more legible handwriting. An embedded video could easily have been replicated years ago with a

VCR. An interactive whiteboard may allow for the instructor to draw on the slides along with some other features, and that would qualify as Amplification.

Uses that are transformative in nature include simulations, activities that could not be done due to time constraints or safety. For example, a war game or simulation can show changes over large time scales. A chemistry simulation can show half-lives of radioactive material, something rather unwanted in a live classroom, or the effects of extremely high temperatures and pressures on a gas, conditions impossible to reach in a normal chemistry lab.

Other examples include the ability to communicate with students around the world, or to collaborate on large scale data collection (such as climate and weather) from various locations around the globe. Students in world language classes can converse with other students through blogs and virtual communication tools like Skype and Google Hangout. These experiences fall under the realm of difficult to achieve without the presence of technology. Further, these include instructional strategies that are key to their respective disciplines, such as the collection and analysis of data, the testing of hypotheses, and frequent writing and communication with native speakers.

Again, replacement activities are not necessarily a bad thing. However, if a district looks carefully at the teachers' uses of technology in the classroom, and the vast majority of them fall in the category of Replacement, it becomes very hard to justify the time and expense to train teachers and purchase the equipment to conduct these activities, as they will likely show no demonstrable gain in achievement.

Likewise, not every use of technology needs to involve complete student-controlled inquiry where the technology use is pervasive and embedded in every single activity. Rather, if teachers are merely using it for their own purposes on an inconsistent and isolated basis, then there's room for change. Further, the technology in the classroom may not be sufficient to consistently incorporate it into student-centered activities. Also, purely student-centered activities may not be the best instructional strategy for the given objectives.

Was it Worth it?

Finally, it is one thing to see students performing better than before, whether it is an increase in reading scores school-wide or if students perform better on a particular unit test where historically scores have been low. However, educators must also consider the costs of time and effort to achieve these gains. Consider the following matrix:

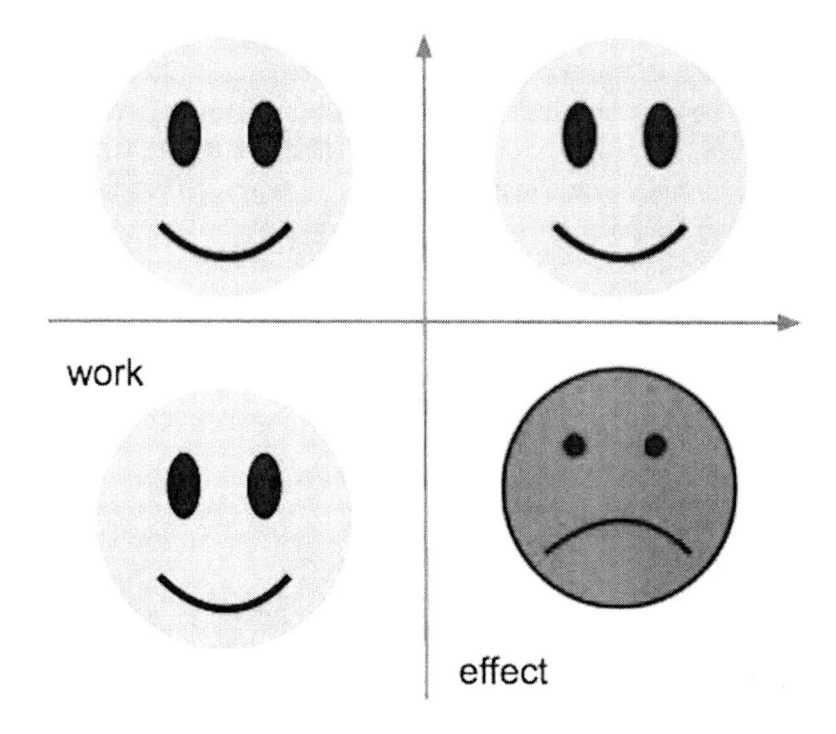

work

effect

When measuring the impact of a new initiative or implementation of a strategy, time and effort must be weighed against the effect of the benefits. If educators are spending endless hours on a strategy that only yields minor benefits, they should question whether to continue. Remember, everything works in education, so perhaps there is another strategy or intervention that works just as well (or better) and requires less effort. Time is important to teachers, and, going back to the first two chapters of the book, it can be considered an ethical decision whether to waste time and resources on an initiative that shows little promise or move on to something that yields better performance with equal costs. Further, time saved can be spent on improvement elsewhere in the school or classroom.

Concluding Thoughts

Earlier in this chapter, I mentioned the skeptical view some teachers may have regarding mandates from administrators who are not perceived to have a solid knowledge of curriculum and instruction, particularly when talking about content specific strategies. As such, leaders would be wise to formulate school- and district-wide professional development around more general pedagogical strategies such as feedback and formative assessment, data analysis, reciprocal teaching, and so on. Time (and accountability for this time) should be built in for subject-area leaders to conduct more focused professional development within individual subjects. Further, the content of this book should also promote a sense of individualized learning in the content areas if teachers work to develop their Personal Learning Networks.

References

Hattie, J. (2008). *Visible learning: A synthesis of over 800 meta-analyses relating to achievement.* New York: Routledge.

Hughes, J., Thomas, R., & Scharber, C. (2006). Assessing technology integration: The RAT—Replacement, Amplification, and Transformation—framework. In C. Crawford et al. (Eds.), *Proceedings of Society for Information Technology & Teacher Education International Conference* (pp. 1616–1620). Chesapeake, VA: AACE.

Conclusion

The purpose of this book was to provide a framework for administrators and technology coaches to instill the value of technology in teachers and foster both personal growth and increased student achievement. It was not meant to solve every problem or provide a foolproof method for bringing every teacher up to speed. Rather, it was meant as a reference point to begin and sustain the discussion about technology, regardless of the state of technology in an individual's building or district.

My recommendation for anyone who reads this book is to immediately think, "next year." The ideas in this book are meant to be conversation starters, and you should spend the current or upcoming school year talking about these ideas and planning for the next year. If you do not currently have one, set up a technology development committee. Explore your current resources; not just what you have in your building or district, but also resources provided by the region and state. Perhaps resources already exist that you can tap into, so you do not have to reinvent the wheel.

My second recommendation is to try not to tackle every pressing problem at once, whether they are previously known problems or issues that come to light after reading this book. My belief is that beginning by dealing with professionalism is always a good idea. This can invigorate staff to approach technology with a clear purpose in mind, while they build their abilities to search for their unique solutions. Then, try to establish school or district-wide initiatives to address singular concerns in the each of the other three areas. Anything more than that would be too time intensive and will likely overwhelm your staff with change...on top of all of the other things teachers must accomplish during the school day.

My final recommendation is to make sure that data are collected and processes evaluated. Linking back to the first recommendation—plan ahead—leaders should not only be asking about problems and solutions, but also figuring out if solutions have worked. Be transparent, and willing to say, "This initiative did not go as planned." Share goals and benchmarks, not only as a motivational tool but also to show that leaders are not continuing failed initiatives for the sake of saving face.

Putting it all Together

One of the "elephants in the room" is teacher evaluations. Our current environment in K-12 education is one where a large emphasis is placed on student performance, student growth, or what some call the "value-add" mentality. There is a controversial discussion going on regarding whether student performance is an indicator of teacher quality. Few other professions are judged by their outputs when those outputs are only under their watch for less than 30% of the day. Lawyers are not judged on how well their clients obey the law while on their retainer. Police officers aren't rated solely on the number of traffic citations they issue, without taking into account whether they work in a rural village or a major city. This argument is a double-edged sword, though. If teachers complain about this environment of accountability, saying that student performance is largely out of their control, then critics say, "Look, even the teachers know they don't matter; let's put less skilled personnel in the classroom so we can pay them less!"

How can a district attempt to improve student performance without leaning on problematic measurements of teacher quality? I would propose that the process outlined in the figure below could be a start. We can look at how the professional development model outlined in this book plays a role in each of the steps, with the shaded area being the sources of evidence for teacher evaluations.

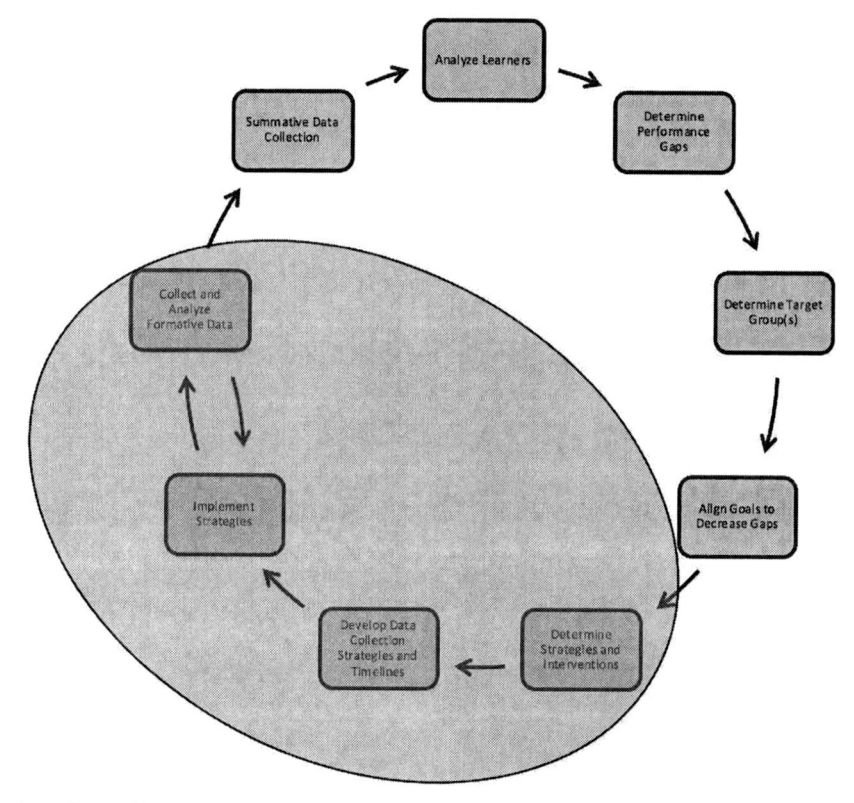

Analyze Learners

This was covered in the Preferment chapter. To recap, this requires more than just looking at test scores, although this does play a role in successive steps. What cultural and socioeconomic differences exist, how do these differences impact performance, and how do they affect technological decisions? Professional development for teachers should involve data collection and analysis training as well as cultural awareness training.

Determine Performance Gaps

At some point, assessment data will likely reveal gaps in performance. This can take several forms. It could be that the school is on a "watch list" at either the state or federal level. What are the reasons for appearing on that list? In other situations, an indicator in one area may be lagging compared to other indicators. For example, while scores are pretty good across the board, a school might notice that their reading comprehension scores, while still good, are lower than their math or science scores. Over time, as the culture of improvement becomes more engrained, the gap identification process can trickle down to the department or grade level and become more specific.

In short, regardless of the specific differences between schools, there is likely a problem or two that needs fixing. However, how should we approach problems that might seem insurmountable? Tackle the high leverage problems first. Things like reading comprehension transcend all subjects and grade levels. Improving comprehension skills across the board should help alleviate more problems than focusing on a narrower topic, as would improving some basic skills like number sense or decoding.

Determine Target Group(s)

Chances are, once the data are thoroughly analyzed, certain subgroups of students contribute to the overall performance gap more than others. This does not mean that schools should only use strategies and interventions for these particular groups. Strategies should be used schoolwide. However, the analysis of these learners should drive decisions for which strategies should be given priority. Technology decisions should also be based on what you know about the target groups.

Please note that this should be a school-wide, grass-roots initiative, not something handed down from an administrator or a small group of individuals. Almost all of the teaching staff should have a role in learning about the data collection and analysis processes. As mentioned earlier, once major problems are solved, smaller problems at the department or grade level can be attacked. Having this experience should help individual teachers eventually apply these skills to their own classrooms.

Align Goals to Decrease Gaps

Here is an example of a school improvement goal tied to a specific gap with a specific group of students:

> *Students in the target group, who are at-risk in the area of reading, will maintain or improve reading comprehension skills in areas of making inferences and synthesizing information as evidenced, in part, by maintaining or improving their score on the [regional assessment] by 5% by [end of academic year].*

In this particular instance, the target group was low-SES students, as determined by the free/reduced lunch list. This group of students has a particular set of traits that influence which strategies should be used, as well as how technology can (or cannot) leverage these strategies, which ties to the work discussed in the Preferment chapter. The staff at this particular school had extensive training in cross-curricular reading strategies, so most content area teachers could aim for this goal. Finally, this goal is also measurable and attainable.

Determine Strategies and Interventions

This phase allows for both general and content specific strategies to emerge. Using the example above, there are some general reading strategies one can use to improve comprehension. However, reading a passage from a science text is different from reading literature or poetry. Thus, having a mix of universal and specific strategies to meet the schoolwide goal is beneficial. Content area teachers can rely on their Personal Learning Network (discussed in the Professionalism chapter) to find effective strategies unique to their situation, or to find out how others in their content area have modified general strategies to make them more applicable to a particular subject.

Develop Data Collection Strategies and Timelines

Technology can and should play a large role in the collection and analysis of data. This phase should rely heavily on lessons learned in both the Professionalism and Productivity chapters. With regards to Professionalism, many teachers will need, and I sincerely mean this, remediation on data collection and statistics, primarily concerning the interpretation of statistical evidence. Outside of finding an average, how many teachers can accurately describe the practical implications of a standard deviation, t-test, ANOVA, or regression? In terms of productivity, technology training on how to enter, manipulate, and share data with colleagues and administrators will be necessary to collect, curate, and analyze the information they collect from their students.

Implement Strategies

This one should be pretty simple. Teachers implement the strategies they develop and collect data at regular intervals throughout the year.

Collect and Analyze Formative Data

As the data are collected, teachers need to work together to discuss what the data are showing, and whether to make revisions based on the data collected. Are certain strategies working better than others? Are they working with certain groups of students better than others? How are the students in the target group progressing when compared to everyone else?

Summative Data Collection

At this point, the rubber meets the road, and some summative data should be collected to determine whether or not goals were met. Of course, this is not the end of the journey, as the rule of the game is constant improvement. If the goal was met, the learner analysis process begins again, finding new performance gaps and new target groups on which to focus. If the goal was not met, the goal is adjusted based on the data obtained.

Documenting Teacher Effectiveness

Looking back at the diagram, the highlighted steps (i.e., Determine Strategies and Interventions, Develop Data Collection Strategies and Timelines, Implement Strategies, Collect and Analyze Formative Data) can become the basis for teacher evaluation. Teachers should take the time to document all of these activities to demonstrate their efforts to meet stated personal and school improvement goals. While some states mandate that a teacher's evaluation should be based on standardized test scores, the process by which teachers work to meet student growth goals should carry more weight. Here again, the usefulness of technology in documenting this process can make a teacher's evaluation portfolio much easier to manage. Thus, steps to help this process through professional development can be linked to topics in the Productivity chapter.

Final Thoughts

At the beginning of the book, I discussed some of the problems regarding technology integration. In particular, evidence is often weak, teachers do not have time to learn about quality technology integration, and there is a lot of "noise" in the form of those seeking profit and those who are successful at public speaking yet have little background in pedagogy. This book does not solve those problems; there is no magic bullet to give teachers extra collaboration time or techniques for shaming keynote speakers into changing their tune. However, just as we can teach children to recognize the difference between reliable and questionable information on the internet, this primer can help teachers and technology leaders begin to see through the "noise" and steer teachers toward ideas, tasks, and curricular decisions that have a higher impact because of their thoughtful use of technology.

The P4 Framework Was Built on the Following Presentations

- Siko, J. (2016). The P4 framework for pre-service and in-service teacher technology integration. In *Proceedings of Global Learn 2016* (pp. 114-118). Limerick, Ireland: Association for the Advancement of Computing in Education.

- Siko, J.P. (2015, November). *A holistic framework for teacher technology use.* Presentation at the Association for Educational Communications and Technology International Convention, Indianapolis, IN.

- Siko, J.P. (2016, February). *Technology and Professionalism: How Technology can Improve the Profession of Teaching.* Presentation at Mercy Tech Talk, Farmington, MI.

- Siko, J.P. (2016, February). *Smart Productivity.* Presentation at Mercy Tech Talk, Farmington, MI.

- Siko, J.P. (2016, February). *Is it Really Working? What difference is Technology Making?* Presentation at Mercy Tech Talk, Farmington, MI.

- Siko, J.P. (2016, February). *Pedagogy Before Technology: A Mantra for Transformative Technology Integration.* Presentation at Mercy Tech Talk, Farmington, MI.

- Siko, J.P. (2015, June). *Frameworks for Thoughtful Technology Integration.* Presentation at Oakland University e-Cornucopia Conference, Rochester, MI.

- Siko, J.P. (2015, March). *Putting the ICCE on a SAMR-y of Technology Integration.* Presentation at the Michigan

Association for Computer Users in Learning Conference, Detroit, MI.

OTHER ANAPHORA LITERARY PRESS TITLES

PLJ: Interviews with Gene Ambaum and Corban Addison: VII:3, Fall 2015
Editor: Anna Faktorovich

Architecture of Being
By: Bruce Colbert

The Encyclopedic Philosophy of Michel Serres
By: Keith Moser

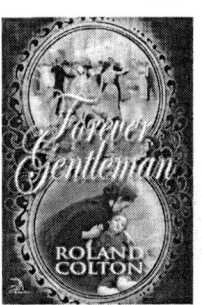

Forever Gentleman
By: Roland Colton

Janet Yellen
By: Marie Bussing-Burks

Diseases, Disorders, and Diagnoses of Historical Individuals
By: William J. Maloney

Armageddon at Maidan
By: Vasyl Baziv

Vovochka
By: Alexander J. Motyl

CPSIA information can be obtained
at www.ICGtesting.com
Printed in the USA
FFOW02n0944171016
28512FF